Be sure to look for these titles in the *Go Parents!* series:

Teaching Your Children Good Manners
will help make teaching your children the
basics of good manners an entertaining and
(relatively) painless experience.

Kid Disasters and How to Fix Them
takes on the common—and not so
common—household disasters kids can
cause, and provides hands-on, common
sense solutions that really work.

"At last, a guide for beleagured parents who want to talk to their children about 'the facts of life' but are uncertain even about how to begin. This accessible and entertaining book provides just the right blend of advice, activities and answers for an often-daunting task. Filled with warmth and humor, it is respectful to the range of parenting styles and to the developmental needs of children. In this sex-saturated culture, where peers and media provide so much of the (mis)information kids get, help for parents is here!"

—Martha B. Straus, Ph.D. Clinical psychologist and author of
No-Talk Therapy forChildren and Adolescents

"I was delighted to read Lauri Berkenkamp and Steven Atkins' new book, *Talking to Your Kids About Sex,* which is truly the best I have read on the subject. *Talking To Your Kids About Sex* provides parents with all of the information they need about what to expect from their children, developmental reference points, frequently asked questions, and exceptional suggestions about the ways in which parents can help their children learn to appreciate, respect, and protect their bodies. Berkenkamp and Atkins present examples and points of information that are masterfully designed to diminish a parent's anxiety in dealing with the questions and issues pertaining to the topic of sexuality. They accomplish this in witty, humorous, and quietly brilliant style."

—Dr. Mary Lamia, host of **KidTalk with Dr. Mary**
as heard on Radio Disney AM 1310 KMKY and AM 1470 KIID

talking to your KIDS ABOUT SEX
from toddlers to preteens

a *Go Parents!* guide™

Nomad Press
A division of Nomad Communications
10 9 8 7 6 5 4 3 2 1
Copyright © 2002 Nomad Communications

The trademark "Nomad Press" and the Nomad Press logo are trademarks of Nomad Communications, Inc. "a Go Parents! guide™" is a trademark of Nomad Communications, Inc. Printed in the United States.

ISBN 0-9659258-3-8

Questions regarding the ordering of this book should be addressed to
The Independent Publishers Group
814 N. Franklin St.
Chicago, IL 60610

Cover artwork and interior illustrations by Charles Woglom, Big Hed Designs
Design by Bruce Leasure
Edited by Susan Hale and Anna Typrowicz

Nomad Press, PO Box 875, Norwich, VT 05055
www.nomadpress.net

For Mom, because reading the instructions inside the box of tampons just wasn't enough sex education.

—LB

To all the proactive parents who are striving to help keep their children safe and healthy.

—SCA

Acknowledgements

I owe many thanks to friends and family who have provided the often-funny, honest anecdotes that are the foundation for much of the book. Special thanks to Lisa Fagan, Leslie Connolly, Susan Hale, Rachel Benoit, and Anna Typrowicz for their stories, ideas, feedback, and edits. Thanks also to everyone at Nomad Press for their hard work and good humor throughout the process of writing, editing, and producing this book.

I have great admiration for Steven Atkins' clinical skills and his commitment to his patients, and loved working with him on this project. Finally, thank you Richard, Sasha, Noah, and Simon for your curiosity, questions, and incredible patience the countless times I said, "Kids, I'm writing this book and I need to ask you a couple of questions . . ."
—LB

I would like to express my deepest appreciation to my current and former clients. I have learned and continue to learn most from you, my teachers. Thank you for sharing your personal narratives, which have strengthened and improved my skills as a clinician. Your stories have touched my life in so many ways and have helped to make me a better person.

To my friends who serve as my chosen family, a special thanks for your endless support and guidance. You know who you are. Thanks also to my family for the humorously embarrassing, yet universally recognizable examples of questions and comments. Kids will and do say the "darndest" things. I also want to thank Alex and Susan and all the staff at Nomad Press. Teaching children about gender, sex, and sexuality can be challenging for parents. The staff at Nomad Press eagerly embraced the task of helping parents in search of such support.
—SCA

Preface

A common clinical concern parents raise in Dr. Atkins' practice is how to deal with the barrage of multimedia messages regarding sex. We have all heard the phrase, "Sex sells." Turning on the television, the radio, or surfing the Internet can result in many unwanted sexual themes. Yet, when looking for guidance, many parents report feeling overwhelmed and powerless.

This book is intended to serve as a guide for parents seeking developmentally grounded examples and recommendations when discussing the potentially anxiety-provoking topic of sex. Readers will discover that the term "sex" has various meanings across developmental ages. "Sex" for a two-year old specifically deals with understanding gender, which differs dramatically from what the average twelve-year old may be wrestling to understand. Discussing the biologically oriented facts regarding sex or gender with your three-year old can help begin the process of open and supportive parental guidance regarding sex as your child ages. This book stresses that parents should be the primary teachers for children and especially with regard to gender, sex, and sexuality. It also offers advice for creating and reinforcing boundaries, teaching children about good and bad touch, and delivering the message that sexual intimacy is reserved only for mutually consenting adults.

The examples offered throughout the book are intended to help clarify how children make meaning of, or understand the world at differing ages. The recommendations are provided to help address sex-oriented topics at various ages. One key theme throughout the book is that of developing the skill of assuming innocence whenever children approach you regarding sexually explicit material. This assumption of innocence entails active listening and supportive guidance since the sexual messages children receive from our culture can be overwhelming and confusing. Children need their parent or parents to serve as primary teachers.

When discussing the various meanings of the word "sex" across developmental ages, certain topics will invariably surface. There may be areas, examples, or recommendations that seem antithetical to rules established in your home. Consequently, you are encouraged to explore your values and to consider incorporating the advice in this book, whenever you deem it appropriate.

Finally, ***Talking to Your Children about Sex*** contains specific questions and examples drawn, in part, from Dr. Atkins' clinical experience. Great care has been taken to disguise identifying information and permission has been granted to use the questions and examples provided. Only the individuals and their families will be able to identify their specific references.

Table of Contents

Introduction

You pick up your seven-year-old son and his buddy after school to take them to soccer practice. As you pull away from the school yard you notice them giggling in the back together. Sensing an adorable, share-with-Mom moment, you say, "What's so funny, guys?" Your son makes a face and says, "We just saw two kids having sex!" And he and his friend collapse into hysterical giggles while you try not to drive off the road. After a couple of deep breaths you casually ask him what he means. He rolls his eyes at you and says, "You know, they hugged and kissed each other goodbye! It was so gross!" As you frantically think of a way to respond, he and his friend start to wrestle in their seats and the conversation is over. You drive on, your pulse slowly returning to normal, and debate whom to call first—the pediatrician or a child psychologist—as soon as you get home.

Sound familiar? Don't worry—help is at hand. ***Talking to Your Kids About Sex*** takes a common sense, practical approach to helping parents talk to their children about a topic that makes many people uncomfortable. Just as no two kids are alike, no two parents will have the same philosophy about child rearing or the same comfort level about sex—or talking about it. This book provides advice and information based on the premise that it's important for your kids to know how their bodies work, and assumes that discussing sexual intercourse and many of the issues that surround sex is a natural, healthy, and important thing to do. This book is also written from the perspective that sexual intercourse is an activity for consenting adults, not preteens armed with ***The Joy of Sex*** and a box of condoms. Please keep this in mind while reading, since your values may or may not correspond to the values presented in this book.

Why Talk to Your Kids About Sex?

Why talk to your kids about sex when they are young? For that matter, why talk to your kids about sex at all? Why—because the information they receive from you is important and will most likely be the most accurate and reliable information about the topic that they'll get for a long time, at least until they begin sex education in school. Sure, your kids will always have at least one friend who will provide them with all sorts of authoritative misinformation about sex and their changing bodies, but do you want to give responsibility for this hugely important topic to children who still think the people on TV are actually inside it? It's also important to talk to your kids early and often so that you *don't* leave sex education entirely to others, whether it's the misinformation of friends or "just the facts" of sex education in school. Your kids learn their values from you, and this is an area where instilling your own values in your kids is vital.

Your parents probably presented you with "the facts of life" when you were well into the throes of adolescence. But consider that talk: by the time you had it (or didn't, in some cases), it was generally too late. You were too embarrassed to ask any questions and you most likely thought you knew the answers, anyway. Taking the same approach with your own children probably won't work any better; and unlike you as a child, kids today are exposed to sex from the moment they can use a TV remote or turn on a computer or radio.

From song lyrics and radio commercials to the most family-friendly television shows, references to sex bombard our kids every day of the week. Parents need to balance that exposure with information that makes sense, is age appropriate, and puts it in the proper context for their children. The earlier you start talking with your kids about their bodies and about sex, the easier it is to continue the discussion as they grow and mature. And the more accurate the information your children receive, the more likely it will help them make informed choices when it matters most. Starting conversations about important topics when they are young shows your children that you are approachable about issues—both large and small—that matter to them. This will become even more important as they grow older.

How to Use This Book

This book should be used as a guide for talking to children from toddlerhood through the preteen years. The information and suggestions for talking to your kids about sex are based on sound developmental principles, as well as on basic common sense. While talking to your kids about sex is, indeed, serious business, it's also exasperating and often very funny—all at the same time. The advice and ideas for broaching this touchy subject are grounded in the belief that starting the conversation about sex with your kids when they are young helps set the stage for open

and honest communication throughout their lives—
especially at those times when it will matter most.
Beginning early also may take away some of the discomfort you might feel: if you can see the humor in the
questions and comments your young kids make while
they—and you—are learning together, you may find it
less agonizing to figure out what to say and when to
say it. If nothing else, you'll all have plenty to tell your
therapists.

Talking to Your Kids About Sex is organized so that you can
either read it straight through, or pick and choose the sections
most useful to you at a given time. All the advice and information
in each chapter is geared toward a particular age level, since you
certainly won't be having the same conversation about body
parts and where babies come from with your two-year-old son
as you will have with your verging-on-puberty daughter.

Each of the first four chapters covers
a different age group, starting with
toddlers and moving through to the
preteen years, covering what kids
will want to know at that age, what
they need to know, and ideas and
suggestions for talking about sex
with them. In each chapter you'll find
a list of games and activities that will
help make discussing particular topics easier for you and your
kids. Each chapter offers a *"Frequently Asked Questions"* section
that looks at common situations and offers practical ideas and
solutions, and a *"What to Expect"* section. *Chapter 5, "Real
Questions, Real Answers,"* is a compendium of the kinds of
questions you might expect from your children—and some answers
to them. The book also includes a list of resources for parents,
ranging from picture books to associations and organizations.

You may be the kind of parent who is comfortable discussing any topic, any time, with any audience. If so, use this book as a reference to reinforce the good dialogue you've already started. If you aren't comfortable discussing sex with your kids (and you're not alone), use the information and ideas presented in this book as a way to jump-start that conversation.

Helpful Hints for Talking about Sex

You don't have to be your neighborhood's answer to Dr. Ruth to discuss sex with your children, nor will anyone refer to you as "those sex parents" if you start talking to your kids about their bodies and how they work. Whether you label body parts with your toddler or discuss impending puberty with your preteen, talking to your kids about sex will take some effort on your part.

1. Model a good attitude: You are your children's most important role model, and the more matter-of-fact you are about the topic, the easier and more comfortable the conversation will be. The more you model the kind of attitude and approach to talking about sex—or any tough family issue—you want your children to have, the more likely your children are to approach tough issues the same way.

2. Keep the lines of communication open:
Your kids may not ask you direct questions about what they want to know, and they may not be asking the question you're ready to answer. Listen carefully to what they say and let them finish their thought before jumping in to head them off before they can go any further.

3. Be patient: Most kids have vague, pre-conceived ideas about sex (and other things) that they may want to talk about, but aren't ready to blurt out right away. Give your kids the opportunity to talk through what they want to know—provide them with prompts such as, "What do you think?" and let them explore an idea with you in a way that makes them feel safe talking about it.

4. Have a sense of humor: Talking with your kids about their bodies and about sex will undoubtedly lead to moments where they bring it up in places where you wish they hadn't. Keep a sense of humor about it: remember that when your four-year old asks you when his penis will grow while you're in the middle of the frozen food aisle, it'll be something you can laugh about when he's an adult.

Loaded Word Alert

Please be aware that the word "sex" in this book will not always mean the act of sexual intercourse. Just as Webster's Dictionary offers six different meanings for the word, from the characteristics that define men and women to the actual act of intercourse, every chapter in this book uses the word in relation to what it means for children of a particular age or developmental level.

1
What's that thing?

Talking to Your Toddler

You've just stepped out of the shower when your two-year-old daughter bursts into the bathroom. She looks at you carefully as you drip onto the bathroom floor, then points to your crotch and says, "Oh, Daddy, what's that thing down there? Can I touch it?"

"No! That's private!" you yelp, and desperately grope for a towel with one hand while keeping the other strategically placed over "that thing." "Let's go find Mommy," you say, wrapping the towel around your waist and escorting your daughter out the door.

After you've put your clothes on and had some time to think about the incident without cringing, you regret not seizing that opportunity to talk to your daughter about body parts and the differences between girls and boys. You promise yourself that you'll say the right thing next time—provided you learn what the right thing is.

The Basics

This chapter will help you discover what the right thing is to say to your toddler, and how to do it. It covers the basics of what very young children are capable of understanding, what is important to teach them, and how. The earlier you start helping your children learn about their bodies and how they work, the more comfortable you'll all be continuing the discussions as they grow older. This chapter will help you learn how to start.

Basic Concepts Covered in this Chapter:

* Labeling different body parts
* Noticing sex differences
* Exploring body parts/self-stimulation
* Toilet training
* Learning about gender identity
* Taking charge of one's own body

It's All About Body Parts: Truth in Labeling

Talking to your youngest kids about sex boils down to helping them learn about their body parts and how they work. While most parents begin labeling major body parts with their children from the time they are babies or toddlers, saying in that sing-song voice, "Where are your eyes, where is your nose?" most stop at the waist, skirt the hips, and come back in around the knees. You don't hear a lot of parents sweetly saying, "Where is your penis?" "Where is your scrotum?" In fact, there's a significant no-man's land from the navel to the knees, usually because parents aren't sure what to call these parts or are uncomfortable drawing attention to them in the first place.

> ### It's Okay to Say It:
> ### PENIS and VAGINA
>
> *What is it about the words "penis" and "vagina" that make intelligent adults giggle and blush like they've never heard them before? As parents, you know what penises and vaginas are and how they work—and the result is standing in front of you. Regardless of the uncomfortable feelings you may have about the words "penis" and "vagina," it's important to use them when you talk to your kids about their bodies—the more you use them, the more comfortable you'll be.*

But now is a perfect—and important—time to start labeling every part of your child's body, using the correct terminology. Forget about "winkies," "woo woos," "wieners," and "down there." Boys have penises and scrotums. Girls have vulvas, vaginas, and clitorises. Sure, they aren't words that roll gracefully (or comfortably) out of your mouth, but neither do "uvula" or "clavicle," and we all manage those fairly well.

Genitals are the only body parts that people have nicknames for, and calling their genitals by other names sends a message to young children that there's something mysterious and forbidden about those parts. Teach your children the proper names for their genitals just as you'd teach them to call their elbows their elbows. After all, now that you're an adult, do you still call your penis a "wiener" or your vulva and vagina your "woo woo?"

Recognizing Sex Differences—
Kids Come with Different Working Parts

If you have small children of both sexes, they will begin to notice that their brother or sister has different parts than they do. Children around the age of two or three begin to recognize that they are either male or female. They do this through categorizing. If you ask your toddler to separate toys into different categories such as size, color, or function, she'll be able to do it. It's the same thing with gender differences. Your toddler will be able to

categorize who is a girl and who is a boy by who has a penis and who has a vulva. You can help reinforce your toddler's recognition of the differences between boys and girls by going through all of your family members one at a time, and asking the same question: "Is Daddy a boy? Does Daddy have a penis? Is Mommy a boy? Does Mommy have a penis? Is Richard a boy? Does Richard have a penis?" (If your child is a girl, you'd probably want to ask the same question using vulva rather than penis.) Your toddler will learn that some members of his family are boys and have penises like him and some don't.

Children around age two or three begin to recognize that they are male or female.

"Daddy, Can I See Your Penis Again?" and Other Embarrassing Moments

As you teach your toddlers about their bodies and the differences between boys and girls, be prepared for those moments when your child might share, loudly, information you desperately wish she had kept to herself. You may not have wanted everyone in line at the bank to know that your daughter saw your penis when you were in the shower together, but now they do. As embarrassed as you'll undoubtedly feel realizing that the person who handles your car payments suddenly knows much, much more about you, it's important that you don't overreact and reprimand your daughter for her comment. Remember that she's trying very hard to understand her world and where she fits in it, and those embarrassing questions are the way she does it. A good way to acknowledge that you heard her and still divert the conversation back to the realm of the not-so-incredibly-embarrassing is to say, "That's right, boys have penises and girls have vaginas."

It's My Body and I'll Stare if I Want To

Between two-and-one-half and three years of age, your children will become increasingly interested in your body as well as their own. Depending on your comfort level, being naked around your children (such as in the shower or bath) will lead to questions and opportunities for explanations about your body and theirs. It's likely that you'll get questions or comments about your body parts: "Mommy, where's your penis? I have a penis." Be aware that you may also get comments like, "Mommy, why do you have a jiggly big butt?", which will probably make you wish your child wasn't quite so interested in your body.

> *"Mommy, where's your penis?*
> *I have a penis."*

If you're comfortable being nude around your very young children, use these times to answer their questions and talk about their bodies and how they are similar to yours. It's not inappropriate for parents to be naked around their very young children; in fact, showing your children that you're comfortable with your body will help them feel more comfortable with theirs.

But I'm NOT Comfortable Being Naked Around My Kids

That said, you may not be comfortable being around your children when you're naked, especially if they are of the opposite sex. If you aren't, don't feel you have to strip down or cavort in the nude so your toddler can learn the difference between boys and girls. Instead, talk to them about their own bodies and answer questions about yours without being naked. It's far more important for you to project a positive attitude about their bodies

than to worry about displaying your own. If you are uncomfortable, it doesn't help anyone.

Why Are They Always Touching Themselves?

Take a toddler's clothes off and he or she is bound to start exploring every part of his or her body, including the genitals. As your toddlers explore their bodies and learn how they work, they are going to discover that touching their genitals feels good—and since it feels good, they'll do it a lot. It's totally normal and, biologically speaking, it's supposed to feel good to touch your genitals. Human genitalia have more nerve receptors than virtually any other body part. Self-stimulation is a normal part of development, and all babies and toddlers do it. You'll need to revise your perception of this activity as masturbation, because it's not—your child isn't touching him or herself with the goal of sexual stimulation, but rather is touching because it's something that feels good. It's important not to shame your child by saying it's dirty or slapping his hand away.

On the other hand, you may not want to hang out on the couch while your son busily tugs on his penis or your daughter explores the crevices of her vulva. Let your children know that it's okay to touch themselves, but it's something to do in private, such as in the bathroom or their bedroom, rather than on the couch while watching TV. You don't have to make a big deal of it, and you

. . . touching their genitals feels good—
and since it feels good, they'll do it a lot.

certainly don't need to go into long explanations—after all, these are kids who can't sit through a five-minute board book. Instead, you can say, "Touching your vulva (or penis) is private touching, and that is okay in the bathroom or your bedroom, not on the couch." To them, it's no different than being told not to eat cereal in the family room; it's just another house rule designed to thwart their fun. Be aware that kids this age aren't able to internalize rules, so you'll have to do a lot of reminding.

Toilet Training

Toilet training looms large in the lives of toddlers (and their parents). While you may half wish you could avoid it altogether since they always seem to need to go just when you are most distant from a bathroom, toilet training presents lots of opportunities to talk—and learn—about body parts and how they work.

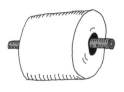
Sitting together in the bathroom reading a book can lead to voiding or bowel movements (theirs, not yours), and the topic of conversation is often about the areas of the body that are uncovered and involved in the

Bathroom Talk: A Toddler's Second Language

You may find your toilet-training toddler spouting "bathroom" talk all over the place. There isn't much that's funnier to a child this age than a conversation about a toilet or a poopy diaper—or better yet, a conversation combining both. Be prepared, because bathroom talk will likely increase as your toddler's language skills develop and he socializes more with other children (who are also busy toilet training and enjoying all the bathroom humor that goes with it). As annoying as it is for you, it really is healthy for toilet-training children to use bathroom talk, especially if they are following through by using the bathroom. Reward your children for letting you know when they have to go to the bathroom, but set limits on how you want them to tell you and what constitutes "bathroom talk" that goes beyond alerting you that it's bathroom time. Similar to the boundaries you set for your kids regarding touching themselves only in a designated room, you can set boundaries here by limiting bathroom talk to the bathroom. This will help reinforce to young kids that it is definitely okay to talk about what their bodies do, but that there are social rules involved about when and where to do so.

action. It's helpful to encourage your toddler to talk about what happens when she urinates or moves her bowels, and what body parts are used. When you do, be sure to use the proper terminology so she gets used to hearing the words and using them herself.

Toilet training is a big deal—your kids are learning how to gain a sense of mastery and control over their bodies, and it's one more piece of the puzzle about how their bodies work that they are figuring out. Remember that it's just as important not to shame your children if accidents happen as it is to celebrate when they do make it to the toilet. Let your kids know how proud you are of their skills while being supportive of slip-ups. Keeping mistakes in perspective on your end will show your kids that you're approachable when other anxiety-provoking conversations and subjects come up at later times in their development. And there will be many.

Gender Role Development: Rambo Versus Carol Brady

Even before your toddler is completely sure what the physical differences are between girls and boys, he or she will begin to recognize what the social differences are between them and start identifying with one or the other. By the time they are three, most kids can tell you whether they are a boy or a girl, and give you a list of things that boys do or girls do—and the lists will probably contain a lot of the stereotypes that make many parents cringe.

Kids aren't born with their gender roles completely hard-wired: they learn what girls and boys "should" do by experiencing the world and watching the people around them. And usually when young kids imitate the behavior that is considered appropriate for

their gender, they get positive reinforcement—which means that your preschool son is more likely to get positive attention when he's playing with blocks than if he's playing with a doll.

Think about the birthday presents you give your children's friends: if it's a boy, how often does, "Barbie" rather than, "exploding truck" come to mind as the perfect gift? Most parents don't make a conscious decision to exclude Barbie and Malibu Skipper from their family room because they refuse to allow their son to play with dolls; rather, it just doesn't occur to them to give "girl" toys to boys, or "boy" toys to girls. That's gender stereotyping in action, and almost all of us do it whether we mean to or not.

So put your money where your mouth is—if you talk about certain values, make sure you show them, as well. For example, if you tell your children that both mothers and fathers do housework and take care of children, make sure you are also modeling this: for kids, seeing is believing. Conversely, if you are watching television, reading a book, or just viewing life together, and you see other people modeling gender behaviors that you don't value, say so—and back it up with your future actions. Demonstrate the behaviors you do value and want to instill in your kids; don't just pay them lip service. It will matter to them now, and even more importantly, it will matter in the future when you'll be talking about more than who has a penis and who doesn't.

Taking Charge of Their Bodies

Most kids love to snuggle and be touched and held by their parents and people who care about them, but the sad fact is they also need to learn what kinds of touching are okay and what aren't—especially from adults. Two- and three-year-olds are very unlikely to understand the consequences of adult actions, and since they are naturally likely to enjoy the feelings they experience when they are touched, they aren't necessarily going to know what's appropriate and what isn't.

It's important to start a dialogue with your children as early as possible about what kinds of touching are okay, and what aren't. The best way to do this is to categorize who can touch what body parts. The only people who should touch your children's genitals are your children; you (when cleaning or inspecting for rashes, etc.); and people who have your permission, provided you are present, such as your pediatrician—and only with your child's permission. After all, it's your child's body.

> *. . . they also need to learn
> what kinds of touching are okay and
> what aren't—especially from adults.*

You can and should talk to your children about this when you are labeling their body parts, during toilet training, or during bath times. Stress that their genital areas—name them—are places that only certain people in certain situations can touch. Realistically, your youngest child isn't going to understand the implications of what you're explaining, but you are sowing the seeds for body awareness and safety.

Games and Activities

Where is Your _____?

This is simply a more complete version of the "Where is your nose?" "Where are your ears?" game. When you are dressing your babies or helping your toddlers put on their clothes, don't jump from their stomachs to their knees and ignore the body parts in between. Be sure to label their genitals as part of the game just as you would their fingers or legs. With older toddlers you can also say, "Where is a private place that no one but you should touch?" to reinforce the idea that there are places that are private and off limits to others. Your kids will have fun, and you'll feel more comfortable talking about those body parts with your kids the more often you do it.

Who Has What?

This game helps kids learn about body parts and sex differences through categorization. Pick a body part or other physical characteristic, and ask your toddler if certain people in your family have this. For example, "Does Daddy have (long hair, nail polish, a mustache)?" "Does Mommy have (long hair, nail polish, a mustache)?" Toddlers love this game, and you don't have to focus solely on who has a penis and who has a vulva—you can play it for any kind of similarities or differences. You'll be surprised how many connections your kids will make that you haven't thought of yet.

Bathroom Talk Game

This game is really more a means of reminding young kids where and when it's appropriate to use bathroom talk, which will help them understand the boundaries you've made about where certain topics are best discussed. When you hear your kids spouting off bathroom talk, announce that it sounds like they're playing the bathroom talk game, and they'd better head to where they are allowed to play it. Often they'll stop using bathroom talk right away, but if they choose to head into the bathroom, praise them for making that choice and allow them to say whatever bathroom-related words they want while they are in there. The minute they step out of the bathroom, though, the bathroom talk needs to be turned off. Usually they get tired of the game about a minute after they've been relegated to the bathroom.

What Can a Boy Do? What Can a Girl Do?

The goal of this game is to help young children begin to understand gender identity and gender roles. You ask your toddler questions about what girls and boys can do, and they answer accordingly: "Can a girl be a doctor? Can a girl be a father?" "Can a boy be a nurse?" "Can a boy be a mommy?" This game is designed to promote the values you want to instill in your child.

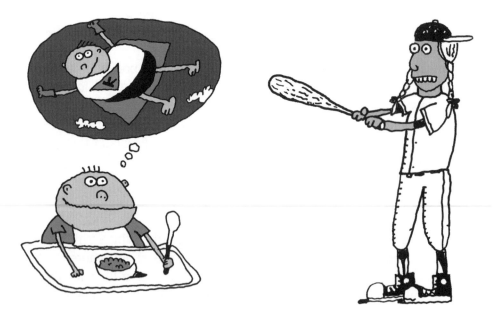

Frequently Asked Questions

Q. My three-year old daughter regularly wanders in and out when I'm showering or dressing. Lately she's taken quite an interest in my body, and it makes me uncomfortable. Is her behavior—and my reaction—normal?

A. *Gender identity is part of natural development and small kids will become curious about not only their bodies, but the bodies of other family members, too— especially parents. Your daughter's sudden interest in your body indicates that she is making connections about the differences between her body and yours, which is an important part of development. Turn these moments into opportunities to talk about the differences between girls and boys, males and females. If you're uncomfortable about your child seeing you naked, shut the bathroom door and redirect her questions to her own body rather than focusing on yours. Now is also a good time to start teaching your daughter about boundaries, so begin to show her that people knock on the door, get permission, and then come into the bathroom.*

Q. My toddler hears older kids using slang like "dick" and "wiener" and "choo-choo" for their body parts, even though at home we use the proper terminology, and now he uses them, too. How do I respond when he talks about his "dick" instead of his penis?

A. *Mimicking words used by older siblings or peers isn't uncommon, but how you react to this will determine how long the behavior will continue. In other words, if you overreact at the mention of the word, "dick," you can bet your child will use it more than once, since he's now responding to your reaction rather than because he likes the word. The best approach is to redirect the child to use words approved in your home without having too strong a reaction. So if your toddler says, "dick," instead of penis, don't yell, "Oh, that's disgusting!" Instead, just say, "In our house we call that a penis."*

Q. I was raised in a household where we didn't discuss sex or our bodies, and we never actually said the words, "penis" or "vagina." I want to raise my daughter to feel comfortable talking about her body and sex with me, but I feel kind of ridiculous using clinical terminology when talking to my two-year-old daughter about her body parts. Does it really matter if I use nicknames for them while she's young?

A. *There are many parents who are not comfortable discussing their bodies, let alone "sex." Your two-year-old daughter will not be scarred for life if your family uses nicknames for her private parts, but it won't get any easier in a year or two or three. Then imagine what it will be like ten years down the road when she needs answers to the really anxiety-provoking questions. Use your judgment and recognize that starting to address the less loaded gender-related issues your toddler is wrestling with earlier will help diminish the more difficult conversations you will be having in the future. Think of this as taking baby steps in preparation for the marathon coming years from now.*

What to Expect from Your Youngest Child

This section gives you some developmental reference points for what your youngest child can understand about her own body. Remember that at this age, sex means body parts and developing a sense of gender.

✓ She will be curious about her body.

✓ She will self-stimulate in many settings (but this is not masturbation).

✓ She may blurt out words or phrases that can be embarrassing to her parents or others, but doesn't do it on purpose.

✓ She will begin to talk about the "potty," which is an indicator that she's learning an important skill and talking her way through it.

✓ She will need you to begin setting boundaries regarding her behavior (for example, no bathroom talk outside of the bathroom).

✓ She will need you to begin setting limits regarding body boundaries (i.e., no one should touch her genitals except you to clean or the doctor to check in your presence).

✓ She will understand her own gender and begin to understand gender roles (and stereotypes).

2
Did You Eat That Baby?

TALKING to Your preschooler

You and a very pregnant friend are having a nice chat when your four-year-old son walks into the room. You notice him looking at your friend's protruding midsection, and say, "Look honey, Staci has a baby in her tummy! Isn't that exciting?" He looks at you, back at your friend, and walks away. A couple of minutes later he comes back and says to your friend, "Staci, did you eat that baby?"

You realize it's time to have a talk about where babies come from before he starts thinking that all mothers are cannibals. But where do you start?

The Basics

This chapter will help you find the right way to start talking with your preschool-age children about the basics of where babies come from and how they are made. You may think your kids are way too young to start thinking about—and discussing—the mechanics of reproduction, but now is the perfect and easiest time to talk with your kids about how their bodies work. Preschoolers are at the unique age where they have one foot in the concrete, experiential world, and the other firmly planted in the fantastic. For them, growing up to be a fireman, Batman, or an invisible magic fairy are all likely, and foreseeable career paths. Nothing is out of the realm of possibility to them. So take advantage of (and enjoy) your children's open-minded curiosity at this age, where questions—and answers—will come more easily and openly than at any other time of their lives.

Basic Concepts Covered in this Chapter:

* Gender stability
* Where babies come from— the mechanics of reproduction
* Socially appropriate language and behaviors
* Body boundaries

The Big Picture—Girls Stay Girls and Boys Stay Boys

One of the most important developmental milestones kids of this age achieve is their realization that girls stay girls and boys stay boys—and that they will grow up to become men and women. While this may seem like small potatoes to parents who have seen some huge changes in their kids—including becoming toilet trained, getting dressed on their own, and not melting down every fifteen minutes—this newfound gender stability will affect your kids' understanding of how their bodies work and how they interpret their sex roles throughout their lives.

It's Not Just What You Say, It's How You Say It

Okay, you've decided to sit down with your preschooler and talk about sex. But boy, you're nervous and you wish you didn't have to have this conversation. So don't—don't try to talk to your kids about sex or their bodies if you're very anxious, because while your child won't understand the cause of your discomfort, he will pick up on your mood and feel uncomfortable, as well. You don't need to put that kind of pressure on either of you, and sitting down to formally have "the talk" when you're uncomfortable about it will be counterproductive. Rather, pick a time when you're enjoying each other's company, and start slow and small—talk about what your son thinks it means to be a boy, and about what he notices about his body, and let the conversation go from there. It's more important to help your children realize that you're open and available to talk with them about whatever is on their minds than it is to cover a certain topic at a certain date. Be an available listener and you'll be rewarded with amazing conversations with your kids both now and in the future.

*. . . the ways the body parts work and why
they are there suddenly become more
fascinating than ever.*

Gender stability will strongly influence your children's conversations with you about what it means to be a boy or a girl in your family, how their bodies differ, and how the different parts work. Your son begins to realize that not only will he never turn into a girl, but also that he won't have a baby when he grows up. Your daughter begins to understand that she might have a baby when she is a grown up, but she will never have a penis. And since they now understand that they'll have the body parts they currently possess all their lives, the ways those parts work and why they are there suddenly become more fascinating than ever.

But Where Do Babies Come From? And How Do They Get There?

An important thing to remember when talking to your preschooler about sex is that for him or her, it has absolutely nothing to do with pleasure or emotion and everything to do with biology and logistics. Forget Victoria's Secret—think animal husbandry. Preschoolers want to know how babies get inside mommies, and how they get back out again—it's the mechanics of the process that interest them.

*. . . you're talking to children who can't
remember which shoe goes on which foot
without regular reminders.*

A great way to start the conversation with preschoolers is simply to ask them where they think babies come from and how they are made—guaranteed they'll have an answer, and you may find they know more than you thought they did. Or they may be completely—but entertainingly—off base. In fact, don't be surprised if you hear your four-year-old son telling you that babies grow in a mom's stomach and then come shooting out of her belly button. Whatever their answer, you'll have a sense of what they know and what they want to know, and the conversation can progress from there.

You probably won't take care of the whole baby-making process from start to finish in one conversation; often kids of this age ask for—and comprehend—only one nugget of information at a time and then aren't interested in pursuing it any further. Be tuned in to when they tune out, and come back to the conversation another time. You may also discover that what you thought you had explained quite clearly received a novel interpretation. After you've explained that babies don't shoot out of a mother's belly button, but rather come out her vagina, you may hear your four-year old telling her friends that she'll be peeing out her baby when she's a grown-up.

Be tuned in to when they tune out, and come back to the conversation another time.

The point is to keep the conversation going when opportunities present themselves, be open to questions the kids may have, and build on the information they have one piece at a time. If you thought you'd be able to have one talk along the lines of, "Well, okay, Daddy plants a seed inside Mommy and the baby grows like a plant inside of her and nine months later a baby comes out her vagina," it's not going to work—after all, you're talking to children who can't remember which shoe goes on which foot without regular reminders. Rather, take it slowly and find opportunities to talk when your kids seem ready to hear, for example, when they are asking other questions about their bodies, about growing up, or even about other people's babies. You'll have started a dialogue with your kids about a sensitive (to you) subject, and your kids will know that you're approachable with the questions they have—which is very important to them.

But What if They Don't Ask?

You may have a child who never asks you a thing about where babies come from or how they are made. And while that might be a relief at the moment, avoiding talking about it is going to make the conversation more difficult as your child gets older. Look for opportunities to talk—if you see a scene on TV together, read a book with a pregnant woman in it, or even see a family with a baby in your neighborhood, take the initiative and ask your child where she thinks babies come from. And be sure to let your child know that she has permission to ask questions about the topic, so even though she may not have anything to ask at the moment, you can be sure she'll start thinking about it.

Getting (Very) Personal

As you have increasingly technical conversations with your preschoolers about making babies and the process it involves, you may find yourself posed with some very personal questions, such as, "When do you make babies?" or "Can I see where the penis goes?" While it can be pretty disconcerting to hear questions like these and difficult to answer them, it's important that you don't overreact. Remember that your children are interested in the mechanics of reproduction in the same way they are interested in how the dishwasher works; it's not personal on their part.

"Can I see where the penis goes?"

The best way to answer young children's questions is to be concrete, honest, and open. When possible, direct questions about your body back to their own so they have a frame of reference. And remember that a picture can truly be worth a lot more than paragraphs of explanation. Have a book available that shows how a baby comes out of a mother so that you can explain how the process works. This will also come in handy when you're answering the question about where the penis goes: you can say, "See here, it goes right into that opening in the woman. That's called her vagina."

. . . your job as a parent is to set boundaries for your kids about what is acceptable and what isn't . . .

Also keep in mind that you don't have to answer questions about your own body that make you uncomfortable. In fact, your job as a parent is to set boundaries for your kids about what is acceptable and what isn't, even when it comes to delving into your private life. For them, it's all trial and error.

It's Potty (and Body) Time! Setting Body Boundaries

This is the age of exploration—kids this age find everything worth investigating, from the interior of the toaster to the underside of every rock in the yard. It's also the age of boundary testing and setting, although they'll be doing the testing and you'll be doing the setting. Kids spend a lot of time pushing the limits of good taste and good behavior, especially around language. Although

. . . the more emotionally you respond to bathroom talk the more you will reinforce its use.

they will be done (for the most part) with toilet training, bathroom talk doesn't end—in fact, you may find it gets worse, even though you may have already established family protocols about when and where it's appropriate. Although it'll drive you nuts, the more emotionally you respond to bathroom talk the more you will reinforce its use. The best way to respond to bathroom talk is calmly to redirect your child to use the words your family has decided to use. When he or she does use the proper words, show how proud you are—a positive response is a lot more fun for both of you.

Now is also the time to set some boundaries for bathroom behavior. You'll probably notice that your preschoolers want "privacy" while they are going to the bathroom, and that's great. Honor that, and from now on make sure they understand that the door should be closed any time they use the bathroom. Conversely, they should wait until someone else is finished using the bathroom or shower before they barge in. Set up some protocols for knocking on the bathroom door when it's closed, and waiting until the person inside has acknowledged the knock and invited them in before opening the door.

The Doctor is In

It can be kind of a shock to walk in on your preschooler and her friend to discover they both have their pants down and one is giving the other a shot on the bottom. While it's not unusual for kids of this age to be curious about each other's bodies and to want to learn about them, they need to know that touching other children's private parts is off-limits. If you discover your kids playing doctor, don't scold them and make them feel ashamed of themselves. Instead, very calmly tell them to pull up their pants and let them know that everyone has private parts that aren't for touching. Then redirect their play. Later you should bring it up with your child and ask her if she has questions about her body and answer those questions honestly and matter-of-factly. You should also talk with the other child's parents about what happened so that they are aware of how you handled the situation. This is a good opportunity to talk with other parents about how they would handle a similar situation. It's always useful to know where other parents stand on things, and whether or not you agree with the way they'd approach various issues. After all, you are entrusting your child to their care when she is at their house.

Don't Look at Me!

Kids around this age may suddenly become remarkably modest—on their own terms. One minute they'll prance around stark naked, telling you that they are a dinosaur and dinosaurs don't wear clothes, and the next they'll be paragons of modesty, telling you to close your eyes before helping them put on their pajamas. Your kids are obviously beginning to make connections between what is public and what is private and will count on you for help and reassurance. So take their cues and help create the support and boundaries that work for them and what you consider important in your family.

*. . . you'll need to weigh their need for
privacy with safety issues.*

You may still be comfortable giving your preschooler of the opposite sex a bath, but if you aren't, or sense that your child isn't, don't do it. Follow your instincts and what's comfortable for you. But remember that you'll need to weigh their need for privacy with safety issues. Even if you aren't sitting directly in front of the tub watching them bathe, you should be very close by—children of any age can still slip and fall in the tub.

I'm Going to Marry Mommy

Another series of boundaries you'll have to help your kids understand are those that involve love and marriage. Four- to six-year olds are learning what love means as well as practicing their gender roles, and to many kids in two-parent families, love equals being married. Go to most preschools and the four and five-year olds are constantly chatting about who they are going to marry or who might marry them—it's like a pint-sized version of the Dating Game without the door prizes. They obviously don't understand what being "married" means—ask the preschooler who comes home and announces he married a tree at school that day—but they are showing that they are beginning to understand

*It's like a pint-sized version of the
Dating Game without the door prizes.*

the concepts of loving and of the social expectations for their gender (except for the kid who married the tree). So if your preschooler announces to you that when he grows up he's going to marry Mommy, don't rush him to the child psychologist: he's giving you a compliment and showing he's becoming aware of his gender role.

And They're Still Touching Themselves . . .

Preschoolers still spend a lot of time touching their genitals, through their clothes or with their clothes off. And why not? It feels good—biologically, it's supposed to. Go to any playground and half the kids there are touching themselves without even realizing they're doing it. For young kids, self-stimulation—which is NOT masturbation, by the way—is a way of soothing themselves. That's all. Your job is not to shame and blame them for this behavior, but rather to remind them where it's appropriate for them to do so. Just as you've made certain places in the house appropriate places to use bathroom talk, let your preschoolers know that if they want to touch themselves in their bedrooms or bathrooms, that's fine—but they shouldn't be doing it in the middle of the family room or at the store.

Teaching Body Ownership: Private Parts are Off Limits— Say, "No!" Then Go and Tell

Your kids may not really know which body parts are completely off limits to others. Tell your son that his penis, scrotum, and anus, and your daughter that her breasts, vagina, and anus, are untouchable, private areas, and no one—including you—should touch them without their permission. At this age, the only real exception is when their doctor needs to examine them, and this should only be in your presence. Likewise, be very clear that other people—adults or children—should not be asking your children to touch their private parts, either.

> *. . . no one—including you—should touch them without their permission.*

Empower your kids: tell them that their bodies belong to them, and no one else. Help your children learn what they need to do if anyone ever asks them to show their private parts, exposes his or her own private parts to your children, or asks your children to touch another person's private parts—no matter what, even if the person tells them it's a secret and says not to tell you. If anything like this happens, your children need to say no and then go and tell you. While teaching your children to do this can't guarantee that sexual abuse will be prevented, it will help your children understand that they own their own bodies and have the right to set boundaries about what happens to them.

SAY, "NO!" THEN GO AND TELL

Games and Activities

Tell Me Again About When You Were Born

Kids absolutely love to hear stories about when they were born, and learning to tell their own story will help them internalize the concepts of how babies grow inside their mothers and of the birth process. Help your preschoolers tell their own version of their birth story by asking them questions to help focus their telling and keep the story going. You'll enjoy listening to them hone both their storytelling skills and their understanding of how they were made.

Do It By the Book

Their baby book, that is. Bring out your kids' baby books to talk about how babies are made. If you have sonograms and baby pictures of your child, use them to help your kids see how babies grow both inside and outside their mothers. If you don't have a baby book of your child, borrow a book about birth and babies from the library, or buy one from the bookstore—your kids will love the time you spend together gathering memories, and will very likely take advantage of the opportunity to ask questions about where babies come from that they might not otherwise pose to you.

Go Down to the Farm

Kids who are around animals can see the cycle of life in action. Hatch a chick; catch some frog eggs; visit the zoo; buy a guppy or a hamster (or better yet, buy a friend a hamster); or go to a farm, and let your kids watch how life begins in the animal world. They'll make great connections between what they see and the conversations you have about how human babies are made and born.

When I Grow Up I'll Be a _____

The goal of this game is to think about all the possible roles your kids might choose when they get older. Each person takes a turn in the spotlight, and chooses what he will be when he grows up: this could be anything from a daddy to a salamander. Other people ask him questions about what he'll do, where he'll live, and how he'll act. This is a great game, and lots of fun, especially because kids this age really believe that they could grow up to be a salamander.

I Spy Someone Loving

The goal of this game is to keep your kids alert to signs of love, respect, and tolerance—and to reinforce the importance of modeling the behavior you want your kids to learn. When you see one of your children do something nice to another, notice it by saying, "I spy Nicholas loving Chris because he let him use his favorite toy." Teach your kids to be on the lookout for moments when people in your house are modeling respect and love for each other. The more you—and they—notice the nice things you do for each other, the more likely they are to continue and internalize them.

? Frequently Asked Questions

Q. I have a girl and a boy, ages five and three. I notice that sometimes my three-year-old boy has an erection in the tub. Is it okay that they still take baths together?

A. *Follow your instincts: if you feel you or your older daughter are uncomfortable, then reconsider having your kids bathe together. On the other hand, if there isn't any anxiety, use this situation as an opportunity to answer questions your daughter or son might have. Every family has its own degree of comfort and you should honor your own and everyone else's comfort level at these times.*

Q. My daughter has never asked me where babies come from, and she's almost six. I don't want her to be shocked when she goes to school and hears from older kids about sex, but I always thought that when she's ready to know about how babies are made, she'll come out and ask me. I think she just hasn't thought about it yet. What should I do?

A. *First of all, don't assume your daughter isn't interested in knowing where babies come from, or that she doesn't already have some (mis)information. Most kids this age do have vague ideas about babies and certainly have lots of ideas about their own bodies. She may feel shy about bringing up the subject with you. Take advantage of times when you're together such as riding in the car, going for a walk, or just snuggling on the couch, and ask* *her where she thinks babies come from. Then see where the conversation takes you.*

Q. My five-year-old son loves to play dress up—and it's not just as superheroes or bad guys. He loves to wear costumes of all kinds, including dresses and women's hats. I'm a little worried about it. Should I be?

A. *This question taps into the gender stereotypes that everyone has. Simply "dressing up" in clothes that break gender stereotypes does not suggest that your child is confusing gender. Nor does it suggest that homosexuality is budding. Remember that kids of this age are enjoying fantasy while moving into a more logical and realistic way of making sense of the world. Avoid shaming your son; rather, encourage him to talk about why he likes to dress up in any of the clothes he chooses, including army fatigues or Daddy's shoes or Mommy's hats.*

Q. My four-year old son and I were at the bank when he announced, "I'm going to have sex with the ATM!" I almost died of embarrassment, but didn't know how to address it. I just ignored it and pretended I didn't hear him, but what should I have done differently?

A. *Know that moments like these happen to everyone. Kids will incorporate new information, like words, into everyday chores. Ask your son where he heard the word and what he thinks it means. Chances are he has no idea what he has said. Remember, your reaction may reinforce his using this word or other words he perceives as outrageous more often. If he senses he is getting increased attention for having said "sex" then he may want to use it more. Try to go about your exploration in a way that lets him know his usage is incorrect. But don't go overboard. Think how you would respond to the use of the word "booger."*

Q. My four-year-old son often plays with a neighbor of the same age. Yesterday her mother called and said she caught both children with their pants down, touching each other's genitals. She laughed it off as kids "playing doctor," but I don't want my son showing his genitals to other children or touching anyone else's body, either. How can I make sure it doesn't happen again?

A. *Now is the time to talk with your son about private parts and who can touch them. Don't shame or blame him for playing doctor with his friend, but make it clear that he shouldn't be showing his genitals to anyone, or touching anyone else's genitals either. Let your son know that you are approachable about any questions he has about his body. You can also proactively avoid situations like this at your house by having a "no closed doors" playdate policy, so you know what's going on during a playdate from the noise. You may also want to reconnect with the other child's mother to let her know how you feel about the issue.*

What to Expect from Your Preschooler

This section gives you some developmental reference points for what your preschool-age child can understand about his own body and how it works. At this age, sex means gender, gender roles, and the mechanics of body parts and how they work.

✓ He will understand that his gender is stable ("I will be a boy forever"), but still believes in fantasy ("I will be a boy salamander when I grow up").

✓ He will be interested in what his body parts do and in the mechanics of reproduction.

✓ He will not be aware of the personal side of sex, or that you might be embarrassed about talking about it.

✓ He will be curious about the world and the rules that govern it, especially as they relate to his body.

✓ He will not understand analogies of "birds and bees," but will understand comparisons between animal behavior and human behavior (for example, seeing a dog have puppies).

✓ He will continue to need boundaries set for him regarding his—and others'—behavior (i.e., close the door while going to the bathroom; no one else should touch his private parts).

✓ He will likely need help cleaning himself after going to the bathroom.

✓ He may want privacy while bathing; parents can respect that but should stay close by for safety purposes.

✓ He will be a concrete learner and will understand abstract concepts when they take concrete, visible forms (for example, love will be understood as hugging).

✓ He will be likely to want to marry you; this is a compliment and an expression of love.

✓ He will self-stimulate (this is not masturbation), and will need to have boundaries set for him about when and where this is appropriate.

EWW, That's so GROSS!

TALKiNG with YoUR 6-9-YeaR OLd

Your eight-year-old daughter is having a sleepover and she and her friends are watching a sappy movie. Ten little girls are bundled in sleeping bags, their eyes glued to the screen. As the hero and heroine move in for the big kiss, there is an ear-piercing chorus of shrieks. One friend pipes up, "Ew, he's kissing her! Now they're going to take all their clothes off and have sex! That is so gross!" All the little girls, including your daughter, shriek again and dive into their sleeping bags, giggling wildly. The scene on the screen changes and the girls pop out of their bags, shushing each other. You quickly head into the kitchen to make more popcorn and wonder just how much of that statement your daughter–or any of her friends–understood and how you'll answer the questions you know your daughter will be asking in the morning.

The Basics

This chapter will help you find ways to talk to children in the early elementary school grades about what "sex" is, their growing (and changing) bodies, and their changing relationships. If you haven't started talking to your kids this age about sex, now is absolutely the time to do it. These kids want facts, facts, and more facts, and as your children move from the early elementary school years of very concrete, rules-based learning to the more murky, hormone-driven world of adolescence, your window of opportunity for communicating with them about important issues will close rapidly. It is a great time to help your kids become aware of how their bodies work now and how they will change in the near future, and what they should know about sexual intercourse.

Basic Concepts Covered in this Chapter:

* Gender constancy and differences
* The social differences between girls and boys
* Dual function of body parts
* The mechanics of reproduction
* Boundary establishment and expansion

The Big Picture: Rules Rule (Even for Santa)

For kids aged six to nine, rules and logic are the name of the game. Kids this age thrive on learning facts and knowing the rules, and the world is very much black and white: if something isn't logically explained, then it can't possibly exist. It's right around this age that Santa takes his last run down your chimney. After all, your eight-year old finally realizes there's no logical way this old guy can make all those toys, know what every kid wants, and get around the entire world in one night. It just isn't possible—which is why so many kids this age switch over into "you don't believe, you don't receive" mode.

By this age kids recognize that their gender is constant—girls will stay girls and boys will stay boys regardless of what they wear or how they act.

This very concrete way of looking at and interpreting the world carries over into how kids view themselves: the sun is setting on the age of make-believe and the contemplation of endless possibilities for becoming a different gender or even a different species when they grow up. Your kids will no longer be telling you they want to grow up to be a butterfly or a ghost. Rather, by this age kids recognize that their gender is constant, and that girls will stay girls and boys will stay boys, regardless of what they wear or how they act. And if you remind them of their earlier plans to live in a fairy kingdom full of bubble houses, they may well look at you like you're nuts and deny it to their grave. It isn't logical, it can't happen, and it's just plain dumb. Duh.

Gender Differences: The Knot versus The Pack

When your kids were little the only thing that was different about them was their body parts; they all played with each other without much regard as to who was a girl and who was a boy. This changes as your kids go through elementary school. Girls tend to gravitate toward girls and boys toward boys during those years, and the nature of their relationships changes as well. Girls are often drawn to more intimate friendships, usually with a small core group of other girls. Their relationships can also be highly emotionally charged, as any mother of a daughter suffering through a "she-took-away-my-best-friend" crisis can attest. Boys, on the other hand, tend to have large, loose-knit groups of friends, and their friendships are based more on activities and

interests than emotional intimacy. Most elementary-school boys aren't clustered in small knots on the playground, talking about how much they like or dislike one of their friends; rather, they are tearing around after each other in a pack, doing their best impression of the final chase scene in *The Lord of the Flies*.

> *. . . girls tend to be talkers;*
> *boys tend to be doers.*

The difference in the way girls and boys act toward their peers matters a lot, especially as you talk with them about their bodies and about sex. At this age, girls tend to be talkers; boys tend to be doers. You may find that talking with your daughter about sex is easy and fluent, and you don't understand what all the fuss is about; you may find that your son never brings sex up at all. Or you may discover that your daughter suddenly turns first to her friends rather than you for information and support, and your son and his friends "talk around" sex by making body-related jokes to each other. ("Trick or treat, smell my butt, take me to the Pizza Hut," while unfathomable to an adult, seems to be a time-tested classic for grade-school boys.)

There's a Whole New World Down There: Multi-Purpose Body Parts

When your kids were younger they were fascinated by the fact that boys and girls have different working parts, and that's about as far as they wanted to go with the information—boys have penises, girls have vaginas, and that's that. As far as younger kids are concerned, genitals serve only two purposes: as terrific fodder for bathroom jokes, and for actual use in the bathroom. But as your kids move through early elementary school, that'll be old news: by the time they are eight and nine, they will very likely be interested in how the parts work, and how they work together. Your kids are beginning to understand that the biology of boys and girls is really very (and fascinatingly) different, and that the process of reproduction involves body parts that before now had only one function.

Kids at this age are ready to know where babies come from, how they are made, and what parts their own bodies play in the process. The best way to tell your kids about the process of sexual intercourse is to start small, and

Beware the "Sexpert"

Your children will always have one friend who has all the answers to all the questions your children could possibly have about sex. Inevitably the information the sexpert friend supplies is wrong, but your kids are at an age when they are becoming more likely to take what their friends say as the truth and bypass talking to you altogether, regardless of how bizarre are the gems of wisdom from the friend. So unless you want your son to think that his testicles will shrink as he gets older until they're the size of dried peas or want your daughter to believe that being in the same room with two boys and no other girls means she'll get pregnant, you'll need to be the sexpert in your house.

be very matter of fact about it. Give only as much information as you think they (and you) can handle at one time. For example, you can say to your son, "Sometimes your penis gets hard. That's called an erection, and an erection is your body's way of practicing in case you decide to make a baby when you get older." If your son seems interested (and is not desperately clutching a couch cushion or making furtive glances toward the door), you can continue with, "When your body changes from a boy to a man, your testicles will grow and begin to make sperm. When you are an adult and if you want to make a baby, you will put your penis in your partner's vagina and the sperm that comes out of your penis will fertilize her egg and help create a baby."

Give only as much information as you think they can handle at one time.

If you want to get the conversation going with your daughter, you can say to her, "Not too long from now you'll get your first period. You'll bleed from your vagina for a few days each month. When you start to have a monthly period it means that your body is ready to grow a baby. When you're an adult and you and your partner decide to make a baby, he'll put his penis inside your vagina and release sperm. That will meet with the egg you produce inside of your body, and a baby will grow from that."

Keep the lines of communication open.

Your kids may have lots of other questions at this news, and if they are talkers, they'll probably ask them—or they might be on information overload or even be ready to die of embarrassment and clam up entirely. The important thing is to get the conversation started and keep the lines of communication open so that their questions—and yours—can continue. Kids want to know what they want to know and tune out the rest, so if your son gets that glazed-eye look while you're droning on and on about the mechanics of intercourse, he's had enough.

Still Touching . . .

Your kids will still be touching themselves at this age, and it's still not masturbation. Rather, you'll probably see them giving themselves a tug or a swipe on the school playground, when watching TV, or even just standing around the house, often without realizing they are doing it. Unlike masturbation, which comes when your kids reach puberty (and sexual maturity), self-stimulation is touching without a goal—it just feels good.

Realizing that their body parts have multiple uses opens up a whole new world for your kids. For your son, it's a revelation to discover that something other than urine will eventually come out of his penis, and he'll have a "Eureka!" moment when he discovers that making sperm is one role for his testicles. (They aren't just for playing with, or storing pee, or any of the other interesting uses he's come up with thus far.) For your daughter, it can be even more enlightening. It's one thing to talk about having a baby, and another to understand the mechanics. Because a girl's genitals are difficult to see, your daughter may not have even known before now that she doesn't urinate out of her vagina, but rather out of her urethra, and that the two are quite separate. Not only is that small vaginal opening the place where she may eventually push out a baby (how will it fit?); but also, and perhaps more significantly, that's where a penis may go to create the baby in the first place.

This is big stuff for kids who may still think of the opposite sex as having cooties and who whine about having to sit next to each other at lunch. It is also not information that you can talk about once and assume they "get" it. Discovering entirely new uses for body parts they thought they had mastered can be scary for your kids—they're learning that what they thought they knew about their bodies was only half the story, and apparently the less interesting half at that. Because it's all such new information, and they hear so much misinformation from their friends, you can't leave the conversation up to their peers alone. Your children will need processing time, and you'll need to be open to the same question posed different ways many times. Be receptive, open, and honest. Above all, remember to be a good and active listener.

It's Not All About the Big Talk

You've been avoiding talking about sex with your kids because the time just hasn't seemed right. But you know you have to do it, so you've set up a time and place for the talk to take place. Living room. 7 P.M. Agenda complete. So here you are, ready to have a heart to heart with your kids, who can't imagine why you're letting them sit in the living room on the good couch or why you're making them miss the Scooby Doo special for no apparent reason. But wait—stop right there. You're making the same mistake most of our parents made when we were young—The "big talk" isn't one big talk. It's lots of little talks, questions, and seemingly random comments that you and your children will make to each other over a long, long period of time. Your goal should NOT be to have the "big talk," but to keep talking—and more importantly, listening— in small doses, throughout their lives.

Getting the Conversation Started

Whether your child is a talker or a doer or maybe a little of both, you'll have to take the initiative to get a conversation rolling—and it's important that you do so. You will find that once your kids start elementary school they will increasingly turn to their friends rather than you for help and support. That means that even if your kids aren't talking about sex to you, they are very likely discussing it with their friends, and are probably getting a serious dose of misinformation.

This is big stuff for kids who may still think of the opposite sex as having cooties.

You may have the kind of kid who has no trouble marching up to you, saying, "Mom, tell me about sex." If that's the case, great—start the conversation right away. However, most kids won't be like this, and you'll have to come up with the best way to approach your own child. If you have very verbal children, be up-front and ask them where babies come from—or even ask them what they think sex is. You'll be surprised at what they'll tell you, and how much of it is wrong, wrong, wrong. If your child isn't a talker and would have a difficult time being confronted with a direct question, don't go that route. Instead, buy him a book that graphically explains reproduction and put it in a place where he is likely to find it, such as his bedroom, on the coffee table in the family room, or even in the bathroom. Let him discover it on his own for a while, and then bring up the book as a way to get the conversation started. That way both of you will have a basis of core facts that you can talk about, and you'll have the book as something to focus on instead of either of you.

Don't Let Them Say, "Yes" and Walk Away

One of the important rules of maintaining a conversation about a tricky subject is to make sure you're asking questions that can't be answered with a simple yes or no. Otherwise, you're stuck with a dead-end conversation like, "Son, do you know what sex is?" "Yes." "Well, okay, then. I've enjoyed our little chat! Let's talk again soon."

Rather, ask open-ended questions that require your kids to respond with more than one or two words. Once you've asked a question, listen to the cues your kids are giving you. Phrases such as, "Tell me more," "Tell me why you think that," "Let's talk a bit about that," help your kids think about their answers a bit more, and will help keep the conversation flowing.

> ### Here are some suggestions for starting— and continuing—the conversation:
>
> ✓ *Tell me how people make babies.*
>
> ✓ *How do you know when your body is ready to have a baby?*
>
> ✓ *Tell me what you think "sex" is. What does that mean?*
>
> ✓ *Tell me how you think your body will change when you get older.*
>
> ✓ *What questions do you have about _____?*
>
> ✓ *Why will your body change like that?*
>
> ✓ *What happens to girls' bodies? What happens to boys' bodies?*

Great Times to Talk about Sex— and Other Touchy Subjects

If you just can't seem to get the conversation started about sex, or it seems to sputter and die after a question or two, here are some suggestions for when to bring up the subject.

In the car: You're focused on driving, your kids are trapped, and you're all in a very isolated, safe cocoon. The longer the car ride, the better your chances for having a valuable and long-lasting discussion.

On a walk: Go for a hike with your kids, and keep moving. It's easier for everyone to talk about potentially uncomfortable subjects if there's something for their bodies to do while their minds are working.

During screentime: Television shows and movies are great times for introducing topics, especially sex, that don't come up in your everyday conversations. The next time a character makes a suggestive comment ("She's so sexy!"); exhibits behavior you do (or don't) find appropriate about sex; or even appears in a way worth mentioning (exceptional cleavage, for example); make sure you bring it up. It's easier for kids to talk about sensitive topics when they don't feel personally on the spot.

With a book: Leave a book around for your kids to discover on their own. There are questions about sex that even the most verbal and talkative child might not be able to ask you. Then when you're having a quiet moment together, such as before bed, look through it together and use it as the focus for your talk or to answer questions. Just as with the television show, your kids can ask questions about what's in the book, rather than about themselves, and feel less personally threatened.

Love is When You Hug and Kiss, Right?

One of the most fascinating and challenging aspects of explaining things to kids aged six to nine is that they are concrete learners—they need to translate abstract concepts into something they can see, touch, or feel in order to understand them, and everything has a definitive set of rules. For these concrete kids, the abstract concept of "love" also has to take very concrete, visual forms for them to understand what it means. If you ask a child in this age group what "love" means, they can tell you what people do to show they love each other—that's how they define the concept.

The most important way you can help your child understand the concept of love is to model it yourself—show them you love them by hugging them; show them that parents love each other by hugging and kissing each other. Tell your children and your spouse or partner that you love them; do nice things for each other; show each other respect and kindness. The intimacy and demonstrations of love and affection you display toward each other will be the most important way your children learn how to show affection and intimacy when they're older. It will also help your kids understand the important role affection and intimacy play in the complicated puzzle of sexual relationships when they realize that sex means more than reproduction. And finally, and more immediately, modeling affection helps mitigate the violence your kids see every day of the week on TV, in movies, and on video games.

. . . modeling affection helps mitigate the violence your kids see every day . . .

The New Boundaries: Respecting Themselves and Others

Just as your kids should already be well aware of the boundaries surrounding bathroom talk, touching themselves, and allowing others to touch them, now is the time to solidify the boundaries around privacy. When your kids are using the bathroom, taking a shower, or changing their clothes, they should be behind a closed door and other people should not walk in on them without their permission. Likewise, your kids should knock before entering a closed door and wait for permission to come in. These boundaries are important not just because you want to avoid the shrieks of, "Daddy, Jimmy keeps coming into the bathroom when I'm in the shower!" They also help set the stage for adult boundaries regarding sex and physical displays of affection. They will certainly help everyone work together through the turmoil of the adolescent years when boundaries and privacy will become paramount and potential sources of tension.

Kids start to notice other children's differences and comment on them— or worse, tease them.

Another type of boundary that you'll need to reinforce strongly to your kids at this age is tolerance for others. Now is the age when kids start to notice other children's differences and comment on them—or worse, tease them. It's very important to teach your children to be tolerant of others, no matter what the situation. Even if you never hear your children being deliberately—or even accidentally—cruel to another child, take the time to talk to your kids about being tolerant of other people's looks, actions, and attitudes. Rather than simply telling them, "Don't tease Dan and say he's a crybaby," or "Stop calling Lillian a fatso," help them put themselves in that other child's place for a minute and realize what it's like to be on the receiving end of derogatory comments or teasing.

Remember that even off-hand comments about groups of people can send a message to your kids that it's okay to generalize and to be intolerant of them.

It's also very important that you do more than preach tolerance—you'll need to model it yourself. Monitor yourself and remember that even off-hand comments about people's sexual orientation, or "women drivers," or even seemingly inoffensive "dumb blonde" jokes send a message to your kids that it's okay to generalize and to be intolerant of some groups of people. It's your job to make sure you're showing your children how to treat all kinds of people with respect. You may never know how much your children will appreciate an open and accepting attitude, but it will make an enormous difference to how they view themselves and others as they mature and develop into adults.

Games and Activities

The Relationship Game

The goal of this game is to help your kids recognize and interpret the appropriate actions in many different kinds of relationships. Read a book or watch a show with your kids, and as the story line develops, think about the questions you want to ask them about the relationships between the characters. After you finish reading or when the show is over, pose your questions to your kids. For example, if they saw a girl and a boy hugging or holding hands, ask them what that means. If they saw two adults kissing, ask them how it is different from a relationship between a mother and daughter. The point is to get your kids thinking about what physical actions are appropriate for particular situations. It's also fun and gives you an opportunity to see how much your children understand about the nuances of different relationships—and has the added benefit of providing you an opportunity to tell your children what's appropriate for your family.

Take a Walk in Another's Shoes

A good way to teach younger children about respecting and being tolerant of other people is to encourage them to "take a walk in someone else's shoes." Have them mentally switch places with someone else and ask them questions based on their own behavior. Do they want other people to stare at them? Do they need someone else to tell them what's different about them or do they already know? What do they want other people to notice about them? This is a game that kids play remarkably well, and you may be surprised at the sophisticated and thoughtful responses they give when they are walking in someone else's shoes.

One Good Turn Deserves Another

This activity helps your kids learn that people who care about each other are sensitive to each other's needs and take care of each other—it's all part of a loving relationship. Do something nice for your spouse or partner, and have the kids be part of it. Buy flowers, clean the kitchen, make a special dinner—whatever special thing you and your kids think your spouse or partner would like. Let your kids participate in the activity so they can also be part of the interaction. Modeling the behavior and attitudes you want your children to have is the most effective way to teach them.

Crossing Boundaries

The goal of this game is to help your six- to nine-year old recognize boundaries of all kinds, including personal space, body boundaries, and behavior and language. You present a situation that involves crossing a boundary and ask what your child would do next. For example, someone is in the bathroom—do you barge in or knock first, even if it's just your little brother? Discussing the possible outcomes of the scenario will give you the opportunity to provide positive feedback to your kids for recognizing boundaries, and to reinforce the importance of respecting boundaries of all kinds.

? Frequently Asked Questions

Q. My daughter is eight, but very young for her age—she never brings up boys or sex, or shows the least interest in discussing how babies are made. I think she'll be a "late bloomer" and it seems way too early to tell her about getting her period or talk about getting a training bra. Will it hurt to wait?

A. *All kids develop at a slightly different pace, and your daughter may not have an interest in her body at this point. It certainly won't hurt to wait to get her a training bra, or to talk about her getting her period. However, don't assume that because she's not talking about sex or her body with you, she isn't thinking about it—or hearing about it from other children her age. You may want to buy her an age-appropriate book about her body and how it works and leave it in her room or somewhere around the house where she'll pick it up and look through it on her own. It may spark a conversation or give her an opportunity to ask questions she didn't think of before.*

Q. My son and his friends make references to sex that I know they don't understand—the other day, one of his buddies said, "Oh, you just humped the couch!" They both laughed, but I knew my son wasn't sure what he was laughing at. Should I explain to him what humping means, or just let it go?

A. *This is a sign that your son is interested in learning about sex and turning to his friends, rather than you, to do so. Find a time when the two of you are together, such as a car ride or a walk, or even while watching TV, and bring up that incident. Use the techniques outlined in this chapter to talk about what humping means. You'll probably find that he has questions, or at least an interest, about many aspects of his body he's never discussed with you before. It's also a great idea to buy a book about reproduction and his body that he can look at and read on his own, then talk with you about. Finally, remind your son about what kind of language is appropriate at different times and in different places.*

Q. My nine-year-old son seems to want to tell me everything about his body. Some of it seems almost too private. How do I let him know this without discouraging him from continuing to share?

A. *What you are really wrestling with is helping your son understand boundaries. Clearly you have allowed him the space to express his interest in becoming a man and let him know it is okay to do so. However, keep reminding him that there are boundaries (like keeping the door shut when a family member goes to the bathroom). Be concrete, supportive, and stay the course of helping him learn what is appropriate sharing and the times to do so.*

So, if your son is informing you every time he has an erection, reassure him that this is absolutely normal and that you do not require these updates. At the same time be very clear that you are eager for him to ask you questions regarding his body or about sex. You don't want him to misunderstand and think he is not supposed to approach you on any topic that he'd like to discuss.

Q. My seven-year old came home with some pretty detailed sexual phrases courtesy of an older child on the school bus yesterday. What should I do?

A. *Get ready, because this won't be the only time your children "learn" lots of stuff from the real world that you wish they hadn't. Remind your children that they may hear phrases from others, but that your family uses the approved words you've developed. You cannot stop the flow of information your children will hear and see, but you can help direct them toward appropriate phrasing and understanding of what they share with you. Be thankful your children are letting you know what they've heard, since it's an indication that you've made their home a safe place for them to learn about sex.*

Q. My daughter has a child in her class with two mommies. She asked me why, and I didn't know what to tell her. Any suggestions?

A. *Yes—be direct and factual. Explain that some kids will have two parents of the same sex living in their home, just as some kids will have only one parent, or perhaps grandparents, or even aunts and uncles living with them. Kids are very nonjudgmental and are not looking for an in-depth understanding of same-sex couples at this age—they just want to know why that family is different from their own. This is a great opportunity to help teach your kids acceptance of differences, whatever those differences may be.*

What to Expect from Your Six- to Nine-Year-Old Child

This section gives you some developmental reference points for what your early elementary school–aged child can understand about her body and how it works. Remember that at this age, sex means understanding reproduction and the various roles of body parts.

✓ She will be a very concrete learner and will want factual information.

✓ She will no longer believe in fantasy (for example, the Tooth Fairy or Santa), and her understanding of the world will solidify as she moves through this age group.

✓ She will understand that her gender is constant no matter what she wears or how she acts.

✓ She will be curious about the duality of body parts (for example, a penis is used to urinate but also to make babies).

✓ She will need you to continue to reinforce body boundaries (i.e., no going into rooms without knocking and permission; no one touching her body or her touching others; appropriate language).

✓ She will be able to bathe and clean herself on her own as she matures through this age range.

✓ She will spend more time playing with children of her own gender: girls will develop core groups that can change quickly; boys pack together and the pack remains fairly stable.

✓ She may be very curious and ask many questions about her body and sex: girls are more more likely to ask questions about sex and their bodies than their male counterparts; boys are more doers than talkers at this age and may need to be approached differently (such as being provided with a book).

✓ She may confuse the rules of gender and sex (for example, she may believe that boys can get periods, too).

✓ She will likely want you to address the same facts over and over again, and may ask the same question several times.

✓ She will need you to be an active listener and provide feedback to her questions many times.

4
I DON'T WANT TO TALK About It!

Talking to Your Preteen

You and your ten-year-old son are in the car, on your way to a "guys-only" night out at the arcade. As you drive to the mall, your son mutters something to you that you don't quite catch. You ask him to speak up, and he mutters it again. You finally say, "Pete, I can't hear you," and he looks at you, wide-eyed, and says, "Today my friend told me that girls start bleeding when they turn 11 and my birthday is coming up and I'm worried about when I'm going to start bleeding, too." You pull into the mall parking lot, hug your son, and realize that you'll be doing more than playing Tomb Raider and making fart jokes with your son tonight—like explaining that boys don't get their periods, for one thing. But how do you start and where do you go from here?

The Basics

This chapter will help. It covers ways to talk to your preteens about their developing bodies and changing relationships with their friends, family, and themselves. It also explains how to keep the lines of communication open as your children are transformed, seemingly overnight, from kids who'd talk about most anything to almost-teens who would rather die than reveal anything to you.

Basic Concepts Covered in this Chapter:

* Sex is not just for procreation
* Pre-adolescence: physical and social changes
* The changing relationship between parents and their kids
* Active listening
* Tolerance and boundaries: social and physical

Moving from Facts to Feelings

As your kids enter the preteen years, they will transition from being strictly concrete learners ("just the facts, please") to becoming more abstract learners. That means that they begin to understand concepts such as love and respect, and the more you model these concepts yourself through concrete actions, the more easily your budding preteens will understand and internalize them.

The Big Revelation: Sex Isn't Just for Making Babies

As your children reach upper elementary school and assimilate all the reproductive information they hear from you, their friends, books, and school, they will also make the connection that the sex that you're talking about and the sex that's on TV, movies, video games, and in music isn't the same thing. Why would someone write a song about a sperm and an egg meeting? Suddenly it clicks: sex isn't just some repugnant act adults perform to make babies; rather, they do it because they like it—apparently it's fun and feels good, too!

> *. . . sex isn't just some repugnant act adults perform to make babies . . .*

Learning that sex isn't just for reproduction is a big shock for kids, because it not only changes the way they view their bodies and how they work (which was already pretty revolutionary, anyway), but can also change the way they view you. Your kids will inevitably come to the shocking realization that you might actually have had sex more times than the number of children you have. Even worse, you might still have sex!

That's why it's terribly important to have already set the groundwork for talking with your kids, and to keep talking—and listening—when the opportunities present themselves. The concept of sex as an expression of love, intimacy, and respect between two people is complicated for kids (and many adults) to understand, and is made more so by the constant barrage of mixed messages your kids receive every day of the week from movies, TV shows, magazines, songs, the Internet, and video games. Sex is often promoted as just another leisure-time activity, like going to an amusement park or eating a really great meal, and your challenge will be to help your kids understand that sexual intimacy involves much, much more than the physical act of intercourse.

A good partner gets his or her needs met without taking away from someone else's needs.

The best way to show your children that adults who are in a sexual relationship also share emotional intimacy and respect themselves and their partners is to model it as much as possible. While your kids will try very hard not to think about the fact that their parents might be having sex with each other, they will notice the way you treat your partner on a daily basis. Show your kids that a good partner gets his or her needs met without taking away from someone else's needs. Let them see that the small acts of kindness and respect you and your partner give each other create emotional intimacy, from giving your partner a quick hug and saying, "I love you," to giving him the biggest piece of pie for dessert because it's his favorite. The more you model your vision of intimacy for your kids, the more likely they are to internalize the same standard for themselves.

When to Talk About Intimacy

As your kids get older, they'll probably be allowed to stay up later, and might be watching more "adult" television programs. Seize the moment when that happens: when there's a television scene showing people being intimate, whether it's a tender hug and kiss or characters wrapped around each other in a steamy embrace, talk about what's happening and use that moment to talk about sex, intimacy, and respect, and how they are connected. Put the focus on the people on the screen rather than on you or your kids, so there's no personal pressure. Also be sure that you comment on both the positive and negative scenes of intimacy that they'll see. You will need to show and tell your kids the values you hold about intimacy, love, and sex—and for good or bad, television shows and movies will provide you with plenty of opportunities to do so.

Tell Your Kids Early and Often: Sex is For Adults Only!

You may feel it's way too early to be making house rules about having sexual intercourse when your kids are only nine or ten, but it's not. Just as the "big talk" is really a series of "little talks," letting your kids know that sex is for adults and saying it now and at every opportunity in the future is important. Nine- and ten-year olds are still rules-oriented and will internalize your values and the rules that stem from them, which will make your job easier when they hit adolescence and the opportunities for having sex actually present themselves.

The Social Picture: Who Am I and Why Are You Still Here?

It won't come as a big surprise to parents of preteen children that their kids are halfway out the door of childhood. The kids who used to come to you with every problem or accomplishment like a nightly newscaster have disappeared behind a closed bedroom door, tittering on the phone to friends. For kids this age, relationships with friends become increasingly important—and will continue to be so throughout adolescence. As your kids reach the preteen years, their focus will shift from you to their friends as a source of loyalty and intimacy. For many kids, this intimacy is, for the first time, on an emotional level. And since all of this intimacy used to be focused on you, you may be feeling a little sad that your daughter doesn't want to have those long heart-to-heart talks with you much anymore. But remember that it's normal and healthy for her to switch her loyalties and feelings of emotional intimacy to her friends, and the key to maintaining a successful and strong relationship with your kids at this age is to shift your role, as well, so that you can be a supportive parent and provide guidance while taking into account, and accepting, your changing relationship.

Trusting your kids also means trusting in your parenting skills.

As your kids enter puberty, they will enter a new stage of their lives, and you'll have to respond to that by shifting the way you approach communicating with them about sex (or any other big issue). Even if you've had a very open and honest relationship with your kids up to now, it has probably been based on your honest answers to the questions they have posed to you. The relationship will now switch: from now on, you'll have to start trusting that your kids will be honest with you and your questions, and you'll need to respect that trust as best you can. Trusting your kids also means trusting in your parenting skills.

Getting Physical: Where Did My Little Girl Go?

Here's something you probably will never be ready for: your daughter sliding into puberty. Girls' bodies usually begin changing around age ten or eleven (although some start as early as nine or as late as fourteen) and you may notice that while just a month or so ago your daughter could easily pass for a boy, all of a sudden she's developing small breast buds and discernible hips. She'll also be experiencing changes you can't see: hair growth on her pubis and underarms, and perhaps even unpleasant-smelling perspiration.

Some girls think all of this is fantastic—they are proud to be "growing up," and will want to talk excitedly with you about the changes they are—and will be—going through. Honor that, and be excited with them. This is a great time to ask them what they know about their bodies and what they notice changing about them, and to answer questions that they will definitely have.

Getting her period for the first time can either be a proud moment or an embarrassing one for your daughter, and much depends on how you approach it.

When Does Self-Stimulation Change to Masturbation?

By the time your kids are in their preteen years, they have internalized enough body boundaries to know that touching their genitals is a private, rather than public, activity. You're not likely to see a lot of penis adjusting or crotch swiping on the playground anymore, since most kids this age are very conscious of the social rules and boundaries that govern public behavior. It's likely, though, that they are still self-stimulating in private. When your kids reach a point in their physical and psychological development when they combine touching themselves with a fantasy, they have transitioned from self-stimulation to masturbation. Masturbation is touching as a means to an end; self-stimulation is just touching. It's probably not a milestone they'll want to announce to you at dinner.

Other girls will not revel in the changes they're undergoing; they may find them confusing and embarrassing. If your daughter doesn't bring up her body changes and you notice them, don't ignore them, and certainly don't assume she doesn't notice them either. Instead, coordinate a time when the two of you are alone but have a common distraction (like riding in a car, working on a project, or even walking somewhere together), and bring up the subject then. Don't make a big deal about how her body is changing, since she'll be very aware of that anyway; rather, talk about how most girls around ten or eleven start to have body changes, and since she's that age, you two had better get ready. For example, your daughter will probably want (or simply need) a training or junior bra. Plan a special shopping trip that might include purchasing one, if she is interested in doing so—the point is to make it a special time focused on your daughter, but not solely focused on her changing body.

Let's Talk Period

Girls used to start menstruating when they were about thirteen or fourteen, but now the average age is eleven, and some girls may start as early as nine or ten. Don't wait to talk with your daughter about menstruation until you think she's close to getting her period; she might get it much earlier than you think, and she needs to be emotionally prepared for its onset. Getting her period for the first time can either be a proud moment or an embarrassing one for your daughter, and much depends on how you approach it. For most kids, the more matter-of-fact you are about menstruation, the easier it will be for her to come to you with questions when she starts. Briefly talk your daughter through the process so she'll know what's coming. Show her what sanitary napkins and tampons look like and buy her a small

Respect your daughter's right to be master of her own body.

supply of her own to keep in her room. You will probably have to explain how a tampon works or at the very least make sure to give her the directions that come in the tampon box. And when she does get her period, honor your daughter's privacy; if she's not the type of kid who wants everyone in the house to know she's begun to menstruate, don't announce it like it's the coronation of the queen. Rather, respect her right to be master of her own body, and ask her if she'd like to celebrate and if so, in what way. Shaving and starting to use deodorant also symbolize puberty and changing bodies, and if you can handle these topics matter-of-factly and without embarrassment, you can help set the stage for more difficult discussions.

Boys Need Attention, Too

Although most boys won't show many physical signs of launching into puberty until they are around thirteen or so (but some start as early as nine or ten), they will need to be as prepared as their female counterparts for the physical, social, and emotional changes that will be taking place. Plan ahead and help your boys get ready for the changes that will be taking place in the near future, because boys at this age are generally doers rather than talkers, and may not know what questions to ask or how to ask them. For many boys, the abrupt changes girls seem to go through can be confusing and disturbing. The same girls who loved to be chased around the playground and treated like pals have suddenly changed into alien creatures who adhere to a whole new set of social rules. It's pretty disconcerting for a kid to realize that the girl who used to play Hotwheels® with him is now wearing a bra and thinks his older brother is hot. Help your sons understand not only the changes that they will go through, but also the changes they see the girls around them going through—and let them know that boys develop later than girls do. They need reassurance that their time will come.

> *He's not likely to tell you about the changes his body is going through on his own.*

Some of the first changes boys go through when they head into puberty are those that most parents won't see—they will begin to grow pubic hair, their testicles begin to darken and enlarge, and they'll have erections more and more frequently at very unpredictable times. They may also have nocturnal emissions, or wet dreams. Any or all of these changes can be scary, embarrassing, or both, for kids if they don't know what they mean. And which is worse for an eleven-year-old boy: to tell his parents he's worried because his testicles are swelling, or that he wet the bed and he's not sure why, but that a dream may have had something to

do with it? Talk to your son about the changes his body is going to go through, so he's prepared for them when they inevitably happen. He's not likely to tell you about them on his own.

Other body changes your son will experience that you can see are increased body hair, from his legs to his face, a deepening voice, and a distinct need to shower regularly. The best way to prepare your son for these body changes is to model taking care of your own adult body so he is ready to take care of his. This means both talking to him about using deodorant and showering regularly—and doing it yourself. It's hard to tell a kid he stinks and should really think about showering when you're walking around smelling like a dirty sock yourself. You may even show him how to shave, even if you're pretty sure what he's calling his beard is dryer lint or leftover cereal. Modeling self care and gender care for your preteens goes a long way toward helping them maintain good personal hygiene habits on their own.

Social and Body Boundaries

Just as your kids should now be well aware (and respectful) of such privacy boundaries in your house as knocking on closed doors and asking permission before coming in, they should also know the social and body boundaries that will become more and more important as they mature into adolescents.

Bumping into kids in the hall, snapping bra straps, pinching someone's butt as they walk by, or ANY OTHER unwanted physical contact is off limits.

Reinforce to your sons and daughters the rule that you've been preaching to them since they have been preschoolers: they own their bodies and no one should be touching them without their permission—and they shouldn't be touching anyone else. "Keep

It's the Worst to Be First

It's really hard to be the last kid in school to go through puberty, but it's no picnic being first, either. The children who go through puberty first not only have the stigma of being different in a sex-stereotyped way, they also don't have anyone to tell them what happens next—it's like being the leader of a hormone-driven safari. If your child goes through puberty early, keep aware of the added dimension of social tension this can cause.

your hands to yourself" isn't something you yell at your kids only on long car rides: it also means that bumping into kids in the hall, snapping bra straps, pinching someone's butt as they walk by, or ANY OTHER unwanted physical contact is off limits. What used to be brushed off as "teasing" and may be hysterically funny to a pack of sixth graders is now officially sexual harassment, and both boys and girls can be victims or perpetrators—and even the most playful or innocently intended incident can lead to unfortunate consequences. So teach your kids to respect personal space, both theirs and everyone else's. And be sure to model this yourself—respect your kids' personal space as you would have them respect yours.

As your kids begin to notice body changes, they may not feel as comfortable with close physical contact with the opposite sex parent

As your kids get older, they will want to spend increasing amounts of time alone, usually in their rooms. Remember that modeling the behavior you want your kids to internalize is the most effective way to teach them: you'll need to respect their privacy boundaries by allowing them time alone, and by showing them the same courtesies regarding knocking on closed doors before entering their rooms that you want them to show others.

Also keep in mind that as your kids begin to notice body changes, they may not feel as comfortable with close physical contact with the opposite sex parent—or you may not feel as comfortable hugging your recently blossoming daughter as closely as you used to, for example. Make sure that you don't back off from being affectionate with your opposite sex child, but rather keep the closeness intact with a level of physical affection you're both comfortable with—take your children's cues and respect the boundaries they set.

"Yeah, Baby!" Preteen Provocateurs

Remember the bathroom talk and acting out your preschoolers used to do? Well, here's Round Two: Preteen Provocateurs. Your preteens are discovering all kinds of new words, outfits, and behaviors and they're embracing them with gusto—probably to your chagrin. From your eleven-year-old son going, "Holy 69!" in front of his friends (or you) when he's impressed by something, to your nine-year-old daughter dressing in an outfit that would make a stripper jealous, provocative behavior can run rampant in houses where preadolescents live.

> *. . . when you're eleven, there is nothing more important than you, you, and oh—your friends.*

It's shocking to hear the phrase, "You're such a whore!" pop out of your beautiful daughter's mouth, or to see your son sporting a scary punker look and attitude—and that's just the point. Kids at

It's All About Reputation

A good way to help your kids understand the implications of their behavior is to ask them questions about their favorite bands, movie stars, or athletes. Ask your kids questions about how their favorite band talks, acts, and dresses: what messages do they send through their clothes or behavior? What kind of reputation do they have? Another way to talk about reputation is to use the role of a parent. Ask your kids what kind of reputation you have (or a friend's parent has) as a parent—how would your kids describe you (or them) as a parent to another kid? How did you (or they) get this reputation? How could you (or they) change this reputation? What would you (or they) have to do? Whether they talk about pop stars or Mom and Pop, thinking about their reputations in relation to themselves and how they treat others will help your kids to develop a positive self image.

this age are talking, dressing, and behaving for attention. It's likely that your kids have no idea of the implications behind the words they are using or the clothes they are wearing. Sure, they know that yelling, "Yo bitch!" or calling themselves (and dressing up as), "party girl" or "hottie" is provocative and (to them) funny. But it's also likely they don't comprehend—or even think about—the ways these choices affect how they are viewed by an audience wider than their peers. After all, when you're eleven, there is nothing more important than you, you, and oh—your friends.

> *Help your kids start to think about what their behavior, language, or appearance says about them to their friends. You'll be helping them see that they are in control of their own sense of self.*

So you'll need to help your kids discover the limits of what kinds of language, apparel, and behavior are appropriate in your family, since they aren't ready to create limits for themselves. Ironically, the outrageous behavior that makes you cringe and wonder if military school takes eleven-year olds really is a sign that your kids are trying out the idea of being grown-ups. But like everything else, being a grown-up takes practice and a sense of where the boundaries are. For kids of this age, what their friends think of them means everything. Help your kids start to think about what their behavior, language, or appearance says about them to their friends or peers, or what messages it sends to them. Ask them if that's the way they want others to view them, or if there are other aspects of their personality that they'd rather be known for. You're not going to stop your kids from pushing the limits of good—or even bad—taste, but by helping them understand that what they say, do, and wear affects how others see them, you're also helping them see that they are in control of their own sense of self.

84

Using Words That Hurt

While lots of your preteens' provocative behavior may seem more irritating than harmful (especially to you), some of it can be quite cruel—especially when it comes to provocative talk. The kid yelling, "You fag!" to another boy who drops a ball during a playground game or the girl hissing, "slut!" to someone she's angry at probably doesn't know what those words mean and certainly won't have a sense of the social impact the words could have—except that they are mean and derogatory, and that was the

> *. . . the best way to promote language and attitudes of tolerance and acceptance is to model them yourself . . .*

goal. It's important to help your kids understand that provocative talk doesn't affect only them and their peers; it's a reflection of how the entire world views them. Educate your kids about the words they use: if you hear your kids using language that is

---

Assume Innocence: Think Like a Kid

You're chauffeuring your eleven-year-old son and a couple of his buddies to a friend's house and you're shocked to hear him say, "I'd definitely date Janet Jackson." You catch your breath and then he continues, "I mean, she could really throw a baseball."

Remember that your kids are still kids—they are thinking about sex, not thinking about having sex. Only a very small percentage of preteen children engage in sexual behavior. So when your kids talk to you or have questions about sex, they aren't asking them because they plan to run out and hop into bed with someone; rather, they ask because they want and need answers—and you can be there to share them.

Tolerance! Acceptance!
Respect!

derogatory, or promotes hate or negative stereotypes, don't let it pass as something "all kids do." Address it immediately: ask them what the word or phrase means. If they can't tell you, explain its meaning and then ask them if that's what they really want to say to or about someone else, or if that's what they would want someone to say about them. Remember that the best way to promote language and attitudes of tolerance and acceptance is to model them yourself and make sure your children do, too.

Peer Pressure: The Good, The Bad, and the Britney

Kids at this age want to be just like their friends—go to any classroom full of fifth or sixth graders and the kids look like little clones of each other: they dress alike, talk alike, eat the same foods, listen to the same music. They are desperate to belong and fit in with their peers. But what's surprising is that while the pressure to conform to the social standard is enormous, that pressure is to conform to pro-social, rather than anti-social behaviors. That means that while your daughter wants to go to school looking like a little Britney Spears or your son wears his pants halfway to his knees because everyone else does, they aren't turning into a gang of rebels without causes or deliberately making anti-social choices because "everyone is doing it." Rather, they are more likely to be ridiculed for being "different" or not following the rules of the school or their social clique.

*You aren't going to turn your daughter
into a walking eating disorder by
acknowledging that she has
concerns about her body.*

While it's nice to know that peer pressure in the world of
preteens is to conform to positive social behavior rather than
negative social behavior, the bad news is that even pro-social
peer pressure can be very hard on kids, especially those whose
body type doesn't conform to the accepted standard. Body image
issues, especially for girls, begin early, and it's very disturbing to
see your nine-year-old daughter look disgustedly at herself in a
mirror and talk about how fat she is, or have your son ask what's
wrong with him, since he's not built like his sports heroes. Don't
avoid talking about body image issues with your kids—if they are
concerned about their bodies, you should be, too. Often parents
say things, like, "Oh, you're just fine," or "You're perfect just the
way you are," because they don't want to appear to be dwelling
on the issue. By simply dismissing their concerns, however, you
may be sending them the message that it's something they
shouldn't talk about—you aren't going to turn your daughter into
a walking eating disorder by acknowledging that she has concerns
about her body.

*Promoting a healthy body image for
your kids means talking about it as
well as modeling it yourself.*

Listen to what your kids have to say about their bodies: if you
hear your daughter say she's fat, ask her why she thinks so. If
your son is worried that he is thinner than his friend, ask him
why that concerns him. Seize those moments when your kids are
giving you entry into their personal worlds and help them discover the answers for themselves.

Promoting a healthy body image for your kids means talking about it but it also means that it's important that you model it yourself. That means you can't wolf down a pint of ice cream and moan about how fat you are in front of your kids. You also need to watch those off-hand negative comments you make about your own body—your kids are listening and watching. If you talk about the importance of regular exercise, make sure you don't consider watching those Bowflex® infomercials your daily workout.

One great way to combine family time and exercise is to do some together—go for a walk or hike, take a swim, play a quick pickup game of soccer, shoot some hoops, or throw a ball around. Get moving and do it together, and it'll quickly become a fun—and healthy—family habit.

Changing the Dialogue: Learn to Be an Active Listener— Bite Your Tongue!

No matter how much your preadolescent children want to be their own person, they aren't sure who that person is just yet, and may not know until they are well into their teens or beyond. Now is a crucial time to reiterate the values and expectations your family has for sexual behavior so your kids can incorporate those values into their own search for identity. And while you can certainly sit your preteen down and say, "Here are our values and we want you to adhere to them," that may not be the best method for kids who are at an age when they bristle at a request to brush their teeth. Rather, the best way to help your children internalize your values while they are working to create identities for themselves is to become a sounding board for them, filtering your values and expectations through the questions about others you ask them and the answers they give you.

More Active Listening Techniques

Here are some phrases that will help you keep the conversation going without you taking over.

✓ *How does that make you feel?*

✓ *Tell me what you think about that.*

✓ *It sounds like you're saying (and repeat what they've just said, then wait for their response).*

✓ *Explain a little bit about what you mean.*

✓ *So what would you do in that situation?*

✓ *Tell me how you'd react to that.*

✓ *What advice would you give your friends?*

✓ *What effect would that have on his/her reputation?*

. . . they need to discover answers
for themselves . . .

This will be a challenge for you and them; after all, until now, you've been "the source" for solutions to their problems, and "because I said so," has worked remarkably well when they've been reluctant to do something you know is important. Now, however, your kids are at an age where they need to discover answers for themselves (albeit with your guidance), and they definitely need to feel that they've reached their conclusions on their own. It's important to remember that your kids haven't tuned you out—they are watching and listening to both your words and actions, even if they don't seem to be.

The Hollywood Method of Relationships

At this stage of their social lives, kids aren't really "dating" in the traditional sense: most elementary and even middle school kids aren't going out together as an unsupervised twosome. Rather, they "go together," which generally means they might hold hands in the hall at school, talk on the phone, or slow dance together at the school dance. Since boys are usually less developed than girls, both emotionally and physically, physical intimacy is usually not a big part of romance in elementary school or even sixth grade.

Most relationships between children of this age resemble business deals between movie stars and their agents more than expressions of true love. Here's how it works: the primary parties' friends act as agents and do all the talking, usually to each other. They reach a deal, and the two love birds are officially "going together," occasionally without ever speaking a word to each other.

One of the most difficult aspects of talking with your budding adolescent about sex, relationships, or other topics that can be touchy, is knowing how to avoid turning every conversation into a mini lecture where you end up doing the talking and they do the listening. Rather, let them discover the answers themselves by facilitating their thought process. You can do this through open-ended questions or comments that redirect them and can't be answered with a simple yes or no. Use phrases such as, "Tell me more about that," or "It sounds like you're feeling XX. Is that right?" to help your kids explore and define their thoughts and feelings on their own—with your help, but without you actually doing it for them. Being an active listener is one of the most important ways you can "talk" to your kids at this age, and the more actively you listen to them, the more open your kids are likely to be.

Parental PsyOps: Depersonalize the Hot Topics

It is far easier for both you and your children to talk about big issues when neither of you is the direct target of the conversation. Listen to your kids when they talk about their friends. Ask your kids what issues their friends are concerned about, and what decisions they are making, and prompt your kids to talk about their own reactions to their classmates' decisions and actions. For example, if you are concerned about the choices your son might make because of current trends in clothes and language, depersonalize it—use questions about kids in general as a way to talk about the issue. That way, you and your son can talk directly about the issue by focusing on other kids. Ask your son questions like, "What do you think Jim wants others to believe or

As you talk with your kids about their friends and the choices they make, you are likely to hear an answer that either reinforces your family's values or goes against your family's values.

think about him by dressing that way?" "What do you think that (outfit, language, activity, choice) says about Jim to his friends? What about other people? How do you think they might see that?" Obviously you don't want to ask your son all these questions at once—you're a parent, not a police investigator, and kids at this age are very loyal to their friends. You'll have to tread lightly. The point of asking your kids questions about other kids is to have an opportunity to talk about how you feel about an issue without putting enormous pressure on your son to talk about himself, or pressure on you to preach a sermon at him. The goal is to help your kids become critical thinkers and make reasonable decisions on their own.

Remember that as you talk with your kids about their friends and the choices they make, you are likely to hear an answer that either reinforces your family's values or goes against your family's values. It's important to use these times to let your kids know you trust them: seize those moments to reiterate your values while always acknowledging to your children that you believe they would make good and responsible choices.

Now is a crucial time to keep the lines of communication open, and to keep the dialogue going about what your kids are doing with their bodies and the choices they make now and in the future.

From now on, your challenge as a parent will be to support your kids' needs to explore their identities and maintain their sense of privacy and autonomy while you continue to convey your expectations and values about intelligent and safe choices, especially about their bodies and what they do with them. Remember that while your kids probably aren't actually getting physical with others yet, they are at an age where sex is fascinating to them and the choices they make now regarding their friends, activities, and image they present to the world will affect the choices they make regarding sex in the very near future. It's a tricky business for any parent, but more so if you've never talked about sex with your kids before now. Now, however, is a crucial time to keep the lines of communication open, and to keep the dialogue going about what your kids are doing with their bodies and the choices they make now and in the future.

Be a Parent, Not a Friend

While you may be feeling a bit left out by the changing nature of your relationship with your child, now is not the time to try to be your daughter's confidante or your son's pal. Kids at this age need strong parental guidance to help them make new relationships with their peers, and they will need you to keep your role

You may never hear your children's friends say, "Wow, your parents are so cool!" (your clothes alone have probably knocked you out of the running for that), but you should take that as a compliment that you're doing your job as a parent well.

as a parent separate and well defined in order to do so. This means not trying to pal around with your kids or their friends on their level, but rather by staying your same old, boring parent self. You'll need to be more, not less, involved in your kids' lives than ever before: know who their friends are, who they talk to on the phone, where they go online and on foot. Your kids are discovering there's a whole big world out there, but they need your guidance to navigate it safely. You may never hear your children's friends say, "Wow, your parents are so cool!" (your clothes alone have probably knocked you out of the running for that), but you should take that as a compliment that you're doing your job as a parent well.

Ideas and Activities for Talking with Your Preteen

What's in a Name?

The goal of this activity is to get your kids thinking about how the words they use affect others. Have your kids write down the names they call other people (slut, retard, or moron, for example) on a piece of paper, then take turns describing what kind of person fits that description. Then have them look up the word in the dictionary and see if the connotation they give the word matches the denotation the dictionary gives it—your kids may be surprised to learn that a word they thought meant one thing means another one entirely. Follow this up by asking your kids what name would bother them most if they were called it and why. Your kids will start to make the connections.

It's Right to Be Civil: Teaching Tolerance

This is a continuation of the "What's in a Name" game, designed to get kids thinking about the reasons behind prejudice. Have your kids come up with stereotypes or common prejudices people have about others and write them in one sentence on a piece of paper. (For example, pretty women are stupid.) Take each stereotype in turn and ask your kids questions about why people might believe them. You probably won't come up with solutions to all the world's problems, but you will introduce to your kids the idea that it is right to be civil.

Tolerance!

Nothing but Net

Your kids may love to be online, but the Internet is the most dangerous tool you could leave a child alone with. If you're not monitoring what your kids are doing when they are online, you are inviting the entire world—not just the nice parts—into your kids' lives. Remember that teaching your kids about sex means keeping sex—and them—safe. No child should have unsupervised Internet access, especially in his or her bedroom. It is your responsibility to monitor where your kids are going online, what they are saying, and what others say to them.

Here are some key safety tips for kids when they are on the Internet:

1. NEVER give out your name, address, phone number, or age.
2. Always tell Mom or Dad if someone online asks for this information.
3. Turn in to the police anyone who asks your children to meet them in person.

Get Involved at School

Your kids will start health class—and sex ed—as early as fifth grade. Find out what your school's sex education class will be teaching your kids, and piggyback your own conversations at home with your kids on what the class covers. Your children may have questions about some of what they learn, from STDs to contraception, that they are embarrassed to ask in front of their friends.

Frequently Asked Questions

Q. My twelve-year-old son keeps asking me to let him watch a popular TV show that has a homosexual theme. I am concerned that it is not appropriate for him to view. Should I let him watch the show?

A. *This is a great question. Parents often wrestle with how to edit out the sexually laden content on TV today, and there are many shows to consider monitoring. Talk with your son about your concerns regarding any show with sexual themes, especially if you feel he is too young to grasp the concepts TV is showing him. Be sure to consider the values your family has regarding sex and sexuality. This book has been written to help parents navigate the sea of messages the media is sharing. However, if you are concerned that your son might "turn gay" if he watches the show, do not be. Remember that a vast majority of homosexuals are raised in heterosexual homes and observe many messages related to and favoring heterosexual lifestyles. They are still gay. The TV show, like any show, can be a springboard for you to talk with your son about sex and his upcoming puberty should you decide he can watch it. It could also make for a great opportunity to teach and model respect and tolerance for differences.*

Q. My daughter is in sixth grade and she prefers to run around with boys who are older than she. Should I keep her from hanging out with them?

A. *Girls often mature sooner both physically and socially when compared to boys. Ask any middle school girl what she looks forward to in high school and she may say "real boys." Monitor your child's movements and actions regardless of how old her peers are. Let your daughter know you care for her and want to make sure she is safe. Even if your daughter says she can take care of herself, she probably does not realize how much she does not know. And you know the world can be dangerous or move too swiftly. So, be a parent. Set limits. Establish a curfew. Get to know your child's friends. Get to know each friend's parents too. If you feel uncomfortable with what you learn, then establish rules for when and how she may spend her time with any particular peer.*

Q. My son says he knows some of his friends are thinking of having sex. What should I do or say to him?

A. *First, take a deep breath. You need one. Try not to react out of fear or panic. It is wonderful he approached you and is potentially signaling that he wants your guidance. See this moment as a compliment to your making it safe for your son to seek you out. He may be talking about his peers or himself. Either way, this is a good time to explore with your son how he understands "sex," and to help reinforce your family's rules on the subject.*

Ask him what he thinks about his peers having sex (potentially). Encourage him to talk with you about how he makes decisions. Doing so emphasizes that you believe he will make good, safe choices. Help guide him as he wrestles with his dilemma—that of "being concerned about his peers." Sex is for adults, mutually consenting adults. Hopefully, your son's coming to you will help reinforce this dialogue.

Q. My daughter made the comment, "I cannot wait to get to high school so I can meet some real men." She has matured quickly, reaching puberty before her peers. What should I say to her about this comment?

A. *A parent's mind can wander down the scariest path quickly. Although her comment may signify sexualized intent, it may not. Boys mature at a slower rate with regard to puberty and social skills. She may be addressing the fact that she feels older and more mature socially when compared to her male peers of the same age. She may feel she understands the world very differently from her same-sex and opposite-sex peers, and is eager to meet others on her developmental and cognitive level.*

Explore with her what she means. Talk with her, mostly listening to what she says, about what it is like as the pioneer of puberty and how she may feel different from others. Ask her what a "real man" means to her. And, if sex is part of that understanding, then explore with her what she is thinking about that topic. Parents want to be, and should be, involved in all aspects of their child's development. This includes the ever-progressing and present "sex talk." Think stages, think safety, and be sure to listen to how your child thinks about sex. We cannot stress enough that a steadfast, concrete rule is that sex is for consenting adults. For a child to internalize this rule requires that parents promote it.

Prepare Yourself for In-Depth Dialog

You may have noticed that our answers to the questions in this chapter are considerably longer than in the previous chapters. This is not by coincidence. Conversations, developmentally speaking, grow longer, with more listening on the parents' part. The complexity with which the transition from understanding gender, then sex, and then sexuality requires more in-depth dialogue.

What to Expect from Your Preteen

This section gives you some developmental reference points for what your preteen can understand about his body and how it works, and about both the physical and social aspects of sexual intercourse. Remember that at this age, sex means sexual intercourse, with all of its ramifications.

✓ He will have an increased understanding, in greater detail, of the biology of reproduction and sexual relations.

✓ He will likely be involved in a sex education program in health class at school.

✓ He will be turning more to his peers for advice and support than to you, but you will still play an active role in listening and answering questions or countering inaccurate information.

✓ He will still look to you to model appropriate behavior, especially those behaviors surrounding respect, tolerance, and acceptance of difference.

✓ He will spend increasing amounts of time alone and will want more privacy as he approaches puberty.

✓ He will need guidance regarding personal hygiene.

✓ He may enter puberty at any time from now through his teenage years.

✓ He may begin pre-dating or talking about dating; relationships may begin and end with little apparent sign of change.

✓ He may be "crushed by a crush" as first crushes happen at this age.

✓ He will most likely talk more about the struggles of his peers and friends than his own.

Real questions,
Real Answers

You're busy cooking dinner while your kids alternately argue with each other and tell you about their day at school. Your ten-year-old daughter is sprawled on a chair at the kitchen table, finishing up her homework, when she looks up from her math and says, "Mom, what's a blow job?"

All conversation stops, as three sets of eyes look expectantly at you while you struggle for breath. The clock keeps ticking, the spaghetti sauce bubbles away, and you wish the floor would open up immediately and swallow you whole. Instead, you stammer something about telling her later, and immediately get everyone to work setting the table and tidying up the family room. Meanwhile you're frantically thinking of what to tell your daughter when "later" comes.

The Basics

This chapter can help. It covers questions ranging from, "What's a tampon for?" to "Why does my penis get hard?" and provides common sense, matter-of-fact answers that you can use as a jumping-off point to start your own discussions. Remember that kids are trying to understand the world and concepts that pertain to it. Sex, love, gender, biology—all these potentially confusing questions can be wonderful moments for parents to teach and direct children.

Please remember that whenever your children ask you a question that you are unsure how to answer, or simply uncomfortable about, be as honest and open as you can. Your kids don't need to know everything about you, and your private life is—and should remain—private. Keep in mind, however, that the questions they ask stem from your children's efforts to understand the world and their place in it, rather than from a calculated attempt to make you cringe.

Keep the Questions in Context: Blow Job vs. Snow Job

It's also important to remember that sometimes what your kids are asking and what you're hearing are two different things: when your three-year-old asks, "Where do babies come from?" she might really want to know the location of the hospital rather than the story of "Sperm Meets Egg: Baby Results." It's a good idea to establish a context for the question, and your answer, before you get started. For example, if your daughter asks you

Clarifying the context of her question will help you understand her level of knowledge and interest.

what a blow job is, you can get a sense of what and why she wants to know by first responding, "Oh, what makes you ask that?" Clarifying the context of her question will help you understand her level of knowledge and interest. You may find out that while your daughter asked you what a "blow job" is, she actually wanted to know the meaning of the word, "snow job," since she read it in a book. Clarify the question first—it'll make a difference to how you answer.

I Don't Know How to Answer Questions Like These!

Answering tough questions doesn't have to cause an anxiety attack. Remember that kids are trying to understand the world and concepts that pertain to it. Here are some helpful hints to keep in mind when faced with the kinds of questions that make you uneasy:

✓ *Always assume innocence when your kids approach you with anxiety-provoking questions.*

✓ *Practice active listening skills, which entails taking a deep breath before answering, and asking gentle, non-judgmental questions to clarify what your child is asking, and honoring your son or daughter for asking you. Remember, your goal is to help your child navigate this world of potential mis-information and to be safe.*

✓ *Respond in a matter-of-fact and positive way. By doing so, you will help create a relationship where your child feels safe about approaching you about sex—and many other topics—and asking away.*

Where does the baby come out? Does the mom poop the baby out?

These are questions that demonstrate what concrete thinkers (i.e., children) will ask. Your child is attempting to understand logically how a baby is born into this world. Be matter of fact and biological in your response. Explain that there is a tunnel called the vagina that's there for making and having babies. The baby comes down through this tunnel and out into the world.

Consider Saying:
Mothers have a special tunnel in their body called the vagina that's for making and having babies. Babies come out of their mothers one of two ways. She will either push the baby out into the world through her vagina, or a doctor will cut a small opening in her abdomen and gently pull the baby out. That's called a Caesarean section.

What is sex?

Here is a great question for a parent to wrestle with but before answering the question, ask your child what he or she is asking. What does he really want to know? You may find your younger kids asking because they heard the word "sex" spoken somewhere. Or, you may find your older children asking because they are beginning to learn about reproduction in school. Remember, try to answer this question and any other on the level your child is asking. Once you have discovered what it is your child is asking, be honest, straightforward and biologically based.

Consider Saying:
Sex means lots of different things. It means the physical difference between boys and girls, it means how people make babies, and it's also how adults express love for each other with their bodies.

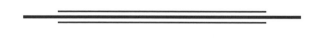

Can I see where the penis goes inside of you? Can I see where you pushed me out of your vagina?

To ask to see your private parts is not an uncommon request. Your kids are trying to understand gender, body parts, and the greater concept known as "sex." Note that your body is your own and that their bodies are their own. Remind them of private parts and state that you are not going to show your penis or vagina because it is your private part. But do get a book out or turn to the back of this book for a diagram and go over the parts of the body. Use the moment to address questions your child might have. Remember, there is a great potential for a lot of mis-information out in the world. This is one of these wonderful times to help clarify what your family is comfortable with and to share the information with your child to help combat any mis-information.

Consider Saying:
My body is very special to me, and your body is very special to you. My vagina is a private place, and I'm not going to show it to you. Let's look in our book and I'll show you where a man's penis goes inside a woman's vagina to make a baby, and where the baby comes out.

When did you make me?

Take some time to gently explore what your child is asking here. Do not assume your child is simply asking for a chronology of his development. He may be asking about how babies are made. So, explore with him what he wants to know but be sure to let him know you are glad he asked. He may want to know about sexual intercourse and how babies are made or he may simply want to know that you carried him for approximately nine months until he was born. Either way, your response should include a comment that you are always eager and happy to answer his questions. Remember, you want to be the teacher of this type of information and to reinforce his approaching you, so not "freaking out" to such a question will increase the likelihood of him continuing to ask questions as he matures.

Consider Saying:
I'm glad you asked that. We made you nine months before you were born. It takes nine months for a baby to grow inside a mother, so we can count backwards from when you were born.

When do you have sex?

Although you may feel like hyperventilating when you're asked this, it's a very common question. You may want to explain that this is very personal and prefer not to answer it. Or you may be comfortable answering the question in a very matter-of-fact way. You may discover that your child may be asking what the purpose of sex is. In that case, explain that sex is for adults, and is an expression of adult love and a way to make babies.

Adults have sex when they want to make a baby, and when they want to express love for each other in a physical way.

How old can you be to have a baby? Can I have one now?

Explore what your daughter is asking. She may truly want a baby now. Sometimes baby dolls don't suffice. Then help her understand the biology of reproduction and if you are so inclined, this might be a good place to begin establishing that sex is for adults. You could also use this opportunity to discuss contraception.

Consider Saying:
A girl can have a baby when her body is ready to grow one. She'll know her body is ready when she starts menstruating—getting her period.

Where do you have sex?

Does this one make your blood pressure go up or what? Remember, assume innocence, and that your child is trying to understand how the world works, and is also honoring you for asking you questions like this. You have clearly demonstrated that you are a safe person from whom to learn. Imagine a child having to ask his peers or someone else these questions! This question, and ones similar in nature, are also great times to help establish boundaries. Don't shame your child for asking, but begin establishing boundaries (like you did with closing the door to go to the bathroom) by noting that adults have sex in private and that it is a very personal way to show how much adults care for one another.

Consider saying:
Adults have sex in private. It is a way for adults to show how much they care for each other.

Why does my penis get hard?
When will it stop?

Boys as young as two will point out when their penises are erect. Imagine not understanding why this happens! Approach this question as another moment of curiosity and wanting to understand the rules of being a boy. Explain that all males get erections and that blood flow to the penis causes the erection. Normalize the response and you may learn he is struggling with getting erections in class. Help him establish ways to conceal natural erections that occur at less-than-opportune times. If he is worried about calling attention to himself, suggest untucked shirts and briefs rather than boxers.

Consider Saying:
When your penis gets hard it's called an erection. It's caused by blood flowing to your penis. An erection is your body's way of practicing for when you're old enough to make a baby.

What does ejaculate mean?

Here is another example of a child hearing a word and wanting to understand what it means. The best defense against a "sexpert" making sexually based words mean more than the biologically based meaning is to answer this type of question matter-of-factly. Your response might include a biological lesson that incorporates ejaculation into how babies can be made.

Consider Saying:
Ejaculation is the release or discharge of semen from the penis.

What is humping? What does fu#@ mean?

Again, here are great moments to help your child understand her world and to help her form opinions of the world. Recognize that your children are trying to understand the world and the sexually related words and phrases they hear. You should help them use the words your family has decided are appropriate. Also, do not expect your child to refrain from using derogatory words if you are using them yourself. Remember, model the behaviors you want your children to demonstrate.

Consider Saying:
These are slang words that mean the same thing as sexual intercourse. Using these words is considered bad manners.

What's gay?

Remember to answer this question in a way that honors your child's curiosity. You want your kids to ask you these questions so you can help form their understanding of the world. This is also a wonderful time to teach the principles of understanding and acceptance. Be concrete.

Consider Saying:
Gay means that two people of the same sex love each other. Another word for gay is homosexual.

How will I know if I'm gay or not? When will I know if I'm gay or not?

Whether your family believes that homosexuality is a choice or biologically driven, what is increasingly clear is that sexual orientation (heterosexual or homosexual) is a sense of inner identity. This topic begs for more than this book can offer. Consequently, we strongly recommend support and acceptance of differences. Homosexual adolescents and young adults are at a higher risk for suicide. If a child asks this question it does not necessarily mean he/she will be gay. It may represent curiosity about how someone knows if he/she is homosexual, and this is a difficult question to answer in a concrete manner. The best answer we can offer you is to say that you will love and accept your child regardless.

Consider saying:
The word "gay" means when a person is attracted to or in love with a person of the same sex—a boy is attracted to boys or a girl is attracted to girls. This is a discovery you'll make on your own when you are older. But I want you to know that we love you and will accept you whether you love a woman or a man. The important thing to us is that you know how to love and how to treat others with respect.

What does cock mean? Why are there so many different names for your penis?

State that there are many slang words for penis, and that cock is one of them. Encourage your children to use the word your family has adopted (i.e., penis) and let them know that using other words is considered bad manners. This question provides another opportunity to reinforce boundaries around appropriate actions and use of words.

Consider Saying:
There are lots of slang words for penis, and cock is one of them. The most appropriate way to refer to your penis is as your penis.

If a penis touches your leg, will you get pregnant?

Here is another concrete attempt to understand the world of sex. Be biological in your response and explain how babies are made.

Consider Saying:
Women get pregnant when their eggs are fertilized inside their bodies by sperm, which comes from a penis. Generally, the penis has to be inside the woman for the sperm to reach her eggs.

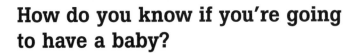

How do you know if you're going to have a baby?

First ask what makes your child curious about this concept. Perhaps he or she is wanting to understand how someone he or she knows is pregnant. Remember, active listening requires asking gentle questions to help tease out what your child wants to know. You just might learn that your child is more confused than the initial question may suggest.

Consider Saying:
To have a baby you need to be old enough to have your period, and then have sexual intercourse. Women know they are pregnant when they don't get their period and also have other physical signs.

What is menstruation?

First ask what makes your child curious about this concept. Is your daughter wondering about when she will reach puberty? Or is your son asking because he heard the word in health class? Exploration will help you address your child's concern. Either way, respond in a biological way.

Consider Saying:
Menstruation is a monthly cycle that prepares a woman's body for possible pregnancy. Every month your ovaries release an egg. If the egg isn't fertilized, your body sheds the lining of its uterus in the form of blood, which passes out your vagina. This part of menstruation is also known as getting your period.

When will I get my period?

Most girls have their first period around eleven years old, but some girls start menstruating when they are nine and others when they are as old as fourteen to fifteen. Not knowing when your daughter will start may be anxiety-provoking for her so help assuage her anxiety with knowledge. Help her prepare for her first period by discussing sanitary napkins, tampons, etc. Go together to buy her first package of napkins if she is willing. Follow her lead. If she does not want to go, then go for her. Also, let her know that every girl is wondering "when" and that every middle school nurse has sanitary napkins in her office and is very helpful if a girl starts at school.

Consider Saying:
Most girls get their periods when they are around eleven years old, but some girls start menstruating when they are nine, and others don't start until they are as old as fourteen or fifteen.

What's a tampon for?

Young kids are concrete learners, and showing them what a tampon is and explaining what it is used for is a great way for them to understand the concept of menstruation and the way a woman's body shows it's ready for pregnancy.

Consider saying:
Women menstruate, or get their period, every month, unless they are pregnant. That means that their uterus sheds its lining because it isn't needed to nourish a growing baby inside. That uterus lining comes out in the form of blood. Women use sanitary napkins and tampons to soak up that blood. Tampons go inside a woman's vagina to catch the blood.

Why don't boys get periods?

Here is a great and very common question from boys and girls. You might be surprised to learn that your son or daughter may believe both sexes will menstruate until they have a health class. Be biological and refer to the anatomical pictures in the back of this book to answer the questions your child may have.

Consider saying:
Boys don't get periods because they can't have babies. They don't have a uterus, which is the place inside a woman that grows the baby.

Why can't boys have babies?

Here again is a great opportunity to help your child understand the wonderful world of anatomy. Refer to the anatomical pictures in the back of this book to help them understands the differences between males and females.

Consider saying:
Boys help to make babies. Boys can't have babies because they don't have a uterus, the special place inside a woman where a baby grows.

What's a blow job?

Here is another great example of a child being curious and wanting to know what in the world others are talking about. Again, take a deep breath and respond in a matter-of-fact way. Note that this is a slang word that is rude and a sign of bad manners to use in public. Set boundaries around appropriate language that your family has decided to use. Try not to shame your child for asking, since doing so may result in her not feeling comfortable approaching you again. Remember, you want to be the teacher who helps guide her through her gaining a better understanding of gender, love, and sex. Let her know you are glad she came to you and then explain the term in a biological way.

Consider Saying:
A blow job is a slang word for oral sex, which is a way of having sex when someone puts his penis in another person's mouth.

What's birth control?

Should you be asked this question, be sure to respond in a way that best represents your family's beliefs. But, be sure to offer honest and factual information.

Consider saying:
Birth control is a term that describes methods for not making a baby when people have sexual intercourse. Condoms and pills are forms of birth control and they are used to keep a baby from being made when adults have sexual intercourse. There are also other methods of birth control, as well.

What's a condom for? I thought it was a balloon. What is safe sex? What is a sexually transmitted disease?

How many parents thought they would have to sit down and explain that making love can be potentially lethal? Although abstinence is the guaranteed way to ensure no one becomes pregnant or contracts a Sexually Transmitted Disease (STD), we encourage parents to explain these concepts to children in concrete ways. We believe that safety through knowledge and information may save someone's life. Be very concrete. We would also highly recommend you contact your local school to learn what the health class is teaching in order to help clarify the curriculum being followed.

Consider Saying:
Condoms (the slang word is rubber) are latex sheaths, like a balloon, that fit over a penis. People use condoms when they want to have sexual intercourse but don't want to make a baby or spread any diseases. Some diseases can be spread when people come into contact with other people's body fluids—and semen is a body fluid. When people refer to "safe sex," they are talking about preventing sexually transmitted diseases. A condom is one way to do that.

Male Anatomy

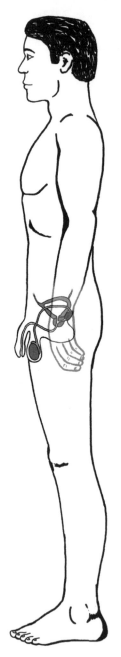

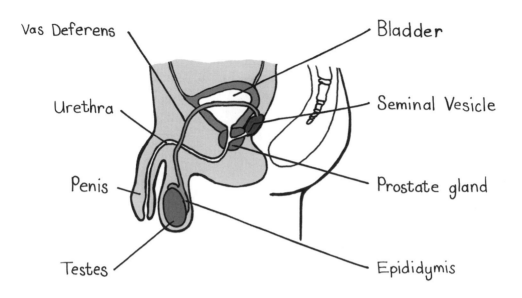

Vas Deferens · **Bladder** · **Urethra** · **Seminal Vesicle** · **Penis** · **Prostate gland** · **Testes** · **Epididymis**

Epididymis – The tube the sperm passes through from the testicles to the vas deferens.

Prostate Gland – Gland that produces a thin, milky fluid that becomes part of the semen.

Seminal Vesicles – Gland that stores sperm and produces the sticky fluid that combines with sperm to make semen.

Testes (Testicles) – Glands that produce sperm (male sex cells) and the male sex hormone testosterone. The testicles are covered by the scrotum, a pouch of skin behind and hanging below the penis.

Urethra – The tube that carries both urine from the bladder and semen from the testes out of the body. (A valve at the base of the bladder prevents urine and semen from leaving the body at the same time.)

Vas deferens – The long, thin tube that transports sperm to the seminal vesicle and the prostate.

Female Anatomy

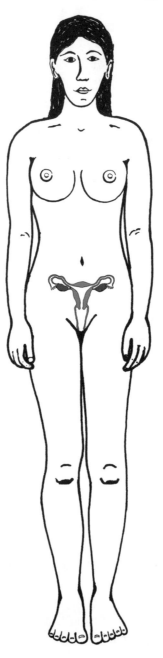

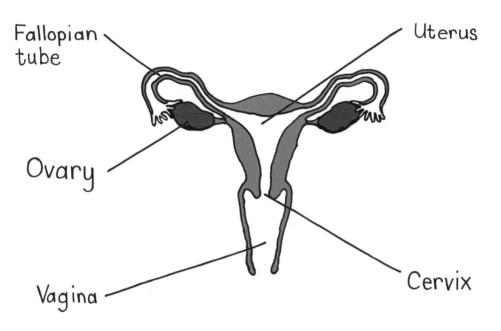

Fallopian tube

Uterus

Ovary

Cervix

Vagina

Cervix – The opening to the uterus.

Fallopian Tubes – The pair of narrow tubes that carry the ovum (egg) from the ovary to the uterus.

Ovaries – Sexual glands of the female that produce the hormones estrogen and progesterone and in which the eggs (ova) develop. There are two ovaries, one on each side of the pelvis.

Uterus – The hollow muscular organ in the woman that holds and nourishes the fetus until the time of birth.

Vagina – The passage that leads from the outside of the body to the cervix, which is the opening to the uterus.

Resources for Parents

BOOKS

Picture Books for Younger Kids

Everybody Poops. Taro Gomi, Kane/Miller Book Publishers, 1993.

The Potty Book for Girls. Alyssa Satin Capucilli, Barron's Juveniles, 2000.

The Potty Book for Boys. Alyssa Satin Capucilli, Barron's Juveniles, 2000.

So That's How I Was Born. Robert Brooks, Aladdin Paperbacks, 1993.

How Babies Are Made. Andrew Andry and Steven Schepp, Little Brown & Company, 1979.

First Comes Love: All About The Birds And Bees - And Alligators, Possums, And People, Too. Jennifer Davis, Workman Publishing, 2001.

Before You Were Born: A Lift-the-Flap Book. Jennifer Davis, Workman Publishing, 1998.

Where Did I Come From? Peter Mayle, Lyle Stuart Publishing, 1981.

How You Were Born. Joanna Cole, Mulberry Books, 1994.

Mommy Laid an Egg! Or Where Do Babies Come From? Babette Cole. Chronicle Books, 1996.

What's the Big Secret? Talking About Sex with Girls and Boys. Laurie Krasny Brown, Little Brown, 1997.

How Was I Born? Lennart Nilssen, (check publisher!), 1986.

Books for Older Kids (8 and up)

It's So Amazing: A Book About Eggs, Sperm, Birth, Babies and Families. Robie Harris, Candlewick Press, 1999.

It's Perfectly Normal: Changing Bodies, Growing Up, Sex and Sexual Health. Robie Harris, Candlewick Press, 1996.

What's Happening to Me? Peter Mayle, Lyle Stuart Publishing, 1981.

A Child is Born. Lennart Nilssen, Bantam Doubleday Dell, 1996.

Books for Boys (8 and up)

What's Going On Down There? Answers to Questions Boys Find Hard to Ask. Karen Gravelle, Walker & Company, 1998.

What's Happening to My Body? Book for Boys: A Growing Up Guide for Parents & Sons. Lynda Madaras, Newmarket Press, 2000.

Books for Girls (8 and up)

The Period Book: Everything You Don't Want to Ask (But Need to Know). Karen Gravelle, Walker & Company, 1996.

Growing Up It's a Girl Thing: Straight Talk About First Bras, First Periods, and Your Changing Body. Mavis Jukes, Knopf, 1998.

Girl Stuff: A Survival Guide to Growing Up. Margaret Blackstone, Elissa Haden Guest, Gulliver Books, 2000.

What's Happening to My Body? Book for Girls: A Growing Up Guide for Parents and Daughters. Lynda Madaras, Newmarket Press, 2000.

Organizations and Associations

Girls Incorporated
120 Wall Street
New York, NY 10005-3902
1-800-374-4475

Formerly the Girls Clubs of America, Girls Inc. has clubs for girls from elementary school through high school. Its web site, www.girlsinc.org, has a long list of parenting tip sheets and resources, as well as activities and information for girls of all ages.

Planned Parenthood Federation of America
810 Seventh Avenue
New York, NY 10019
212-541-7800
www.plannedparenthood.org

The world's largest reproductive health care and family planning organization, Planned Parenthood offers information about a wide variety of family planning issues, including pregnancy, birth control, and sexually transmitted diseases.

PFLAG
Parents, Families and Friends of Lesbians and Gays
1726 M Street, NW Suite 400 Washington, DC 20036
ph: 202.467.8180 fx: 202.467.8194
www.pflag.org
This is a national organization devoted to supporting parents and families of gay and lesbian children.

About the Authors

Lauri Berkenkamp

Lauri Berkenkamp lives with her husband and four children in Vermont. Lauri holds a Masters degree in English Literature from the University of Vermont and is a former faculty member of Vermont College of Norwich University in Montpelier, VT. She is the author of *"Mom, the Toilet's Clogged!" Kid Disasters and How to Fix Them*, and the co-author of *Teaching Your Children Good Manners* (2001) as well as several other books.

Steven C. Atkins, Psy.D.

Steven C. Atkins, Psy.D. is a licensed psychologist, instructor, and clinical associate at Dartmouth Medical School's Department of Child Psychiatry, specializing in specific learning disabilities, ADHD, and developmental theory. He holds a Masters Degree in Education from Harvard University and a Doctorate of Psychology from the Massachusetts School of Professional Psychology. His practice focuses on family therapy and community counseling, including working with children in area schools on impulse control and social skills development. Dr. Atkins serves as a member of the Ethics Committee for the New Hampshire Psychological Association and is a member of the American Red Cross' Mental Health Network, which entails responding to the needs of those surviving national disasters. Dr. Atkins lives in the Upper Valley of New Hampshire.